At Home and Away

Edited by Jeanne Carswell

The production of this book would not have been possible without financial assistance from the advertisers and subscribers whose names appear at the end of this book. We hope readers will support those who supported us.

Thanks also go to:

Castle Donington Historical Society

Ibstock Community College

Ivanhoe Community College

Leicestershire Libraries

Measham Community Office

Mick and Albert - North West Leicestershire Link Van

North West Leicestershire District Council

The Springboard Centre (Coalville) Ltd

Village Arts - Castle Donington

Contributors who lent photographs and documents

Mr T A Grundy for lending his collection of The Billet newsletter

Amanda 'the rigger' Marsden

Everyone who contributed their precious memories

Typing: Linda Green, Vivien Parry, Steve Peace, Jeanne Carswell

Tape transcriptions: Martin Hall, Steve Duckworth, Steve Peace

Typesetting: Steve Duckworth

Front Cover: *Geoff Duckworth, on the left 'At Home' in the 28th (Clutsom & Kemp) Coalville platoon Home Guard, 1940; and on the right 'Away' in the Royal Navy at Port Said, 1943.*

Back Cover: *Based on the cover of the Christmas supplement of the Billet, 1945.*

Copyright © 1995: Coalville Publishing Co Ltd

The Springboard Centre

Mantle Lane

Coalville

Leicestershire

LE67 3DW

Telephone 01530 839531

ISBN: 1 872479 35 9

Printed at Alden Press Limited, Oxford and Northampton, Great Britain

Introduction

North West Leicestershire Arts Council and the publishers intend this book to be a tribute to the role the men and women of the district played in the Second World War. The response to the request for memories was so good that, unfortunately, space does not allow for all the contributions to be included.

Most people chose to remember the lighter side of life during the period so we are especially indebted to those who were brave enough to recall what must have been for them a difficult and harrowing time.

A unique feature for the area was the production of The Billet, a newsletter designed to keep those serving away in touch with their family and friends at home. Some extracts from The Billet are included towards the end of the book.

Tell us about the war Grandad
When you were in the Home Guard
And how you had a stirrup pump
And a shelter in the back yard
Tell us about the barrage balloon
And the Ack-Ack battery
Whatever did it taste like
Having dried egg for your tea?

Why was Grandma in munitions?
With a turban on her head
Tell us about the awful days
You only had lard on your bread
Did you listen to Lord Haw Haw
Or wear a siren suit?
I knew you carried a gas mask
And never saw any fruit

Why didn't you like the Americans
If can't be because they chewed gum?
Why did you threaten to shoot one
If you saw him talking to Mum?
I know Mum used sugar and water
To try to set her hair
And she never had any nylons
Till the American brought a pair

You say you dug for victory
Drank tea with condensed milk
And someone gave Gran a petticoat
Made out of parachute silk
You're very quiet Grandad
And your mouth has gone all tight
Tell us about the war Grandad
I could listen here all night.

Joyce Collins

1

Ron Bombroff

At the outbreak of the Second World War I was 8 years old and lived in Loughborough. My Dad worked at Herbert Morris's after being unemployed. My parents had planned to go on holiday and I was really looking forward to going on this holiday.

With the outbreak of war people were restricted in going away from their homes, so we had to cancel the holiday and I never got to see the sea.

One day while we were in the classroom at school a vehicle moved into the playground. Not long after the headmistress's secretary came to the class room and told the teacher we'd got to assemble in the school hall. We wondered what it was about. In the hall was a desk with all boxes and people behind it. We had to go in alphabetical order and sit at the table and shout our names out to the people behind the desk. When we said our name the people gave us a box. I undid the box and inside was the gas mask.

I?d never seen one before but they never told me how to put it on. It was new rubber with french chalk. The one I put on had a bit of french chalk and when I too a breath I sucked in some french chalk. It made me feel very bad; the lady behind the desk took the mask off me and gave me an arrowroot sweet to suck to get rid of the taste.

I was told to take great care of it and not leave it lying around. One day, the air-raid siren went and we had to assemble outside the class. But me, being a bit awkward, messed about and the teacher asked me where my gas mask was. I said "Sorry teacher, I left my gas mask in the cloakroom." So I had to go back down and fetch it and then meet them in the shelter. But me, I took my time and got my gas mask. When the teacher saw me she got me by the scruff of the neck, clouted me across the back of the head, and was very mad with me.

We started walking through the playground and as we were walking there was action over towards Derby, we could see the balloons. While we walked there was an aircraft coming towards us and it was an enemy aircraft with a fighter following it; so we started running across to the shelters. The fighter aimed for the bomber and some of the bullets strayed. Close-by, in the next field from the shelter, was some horses. Some of the tracers hit on the ground and frightened the horses and one horse tried to jump the fence which was a very spiky one. He couldn't quite jump it so the spikes stuck underneath the stomach, and you can guess what sort of mess it was.

I joined the scouts and one of the things we did was to go round the houses collecting rubber. Bathing hats, rubber rings, rubber gloves, inner tubes, you name it, we went round with the barrow.

We helped the Red Cross collecting books and magazines that went to the prisoners of war overseas.

Frank Moore

1940/41 saw the arrival of Italian prisoners of war in Britain to do agricultural work, and so augment our home produced food supplies. The first time I saw POWs was in the spring of 1941, working in fields at Common Hill, Ibstock. The German war prisoners, taken after the end of the North African campaign, in 1943 and the Normandy landings, were kept in more secure accommodation until the final stages of the war. The first German POWs, I saw personally, were engaged in snow clearing during the 1945/46 winters.

Another occurrence that caused eyebrows to be raised was the arrival of the American GIs, during 1943 and 1944. To a generation such as ours, brought up on American films, dance bands and singers, we associated all of these gum-sucking, affluent, smartly uniformed, khaki clad individuals with the silver screen. However, one member of the Coalville populace soon discovered the traits of the devil-may-care gum-sucking GIs could be turned to one's financial advantage.

There were two Liberty Trucks which arrived in Coalville every Friday night, from the American camp near Burton-on-Trent, to give the GIs recreational and female entertainment at the local dance halls. The favourite haunt was soon to become the Engineers Arms where a certain 'local' soon had the GIs parting with cigarettes, candy and many other items, so readily obtainable to them in the US Army PX canteens, without restriction. In return, our local entrepreneur was able to supply his friends with this contraband. However, he became too ambitious when he promised some of his American friends bottles of the 'real McCoy' - Scotch Whisky, at five pounds per bottle. Of course, he found it so easy to promise the whisky and take the fivers, but not so easy to supply the whisky. His customers soon became restless at the length of time they had to wait for delivery. Threats were made and so he was forced to beat an hasty retreat and pray for D.Day.

Memories from members of the Castle Donington Historical Society including Geraldine Hallam, June Lester, Margaret Lindner, Tom Pegg and Bruce Townsend.

I can remember prisoners of war at Melbourne working in the gardens at the back of my grandma's house. There was market garden land at the back. I was about three or four years old. They were probably billeted at Staunton Harold Hall. There were Italians to start with followed by Germans. They wore brown uniforms with bright patches.

I can remember my dad taking me up to the Observer Corps platform which was on the cricket pitch. It was a big wooden structure up a lot of steps. It was just a square with half of it covered in at the top with an open platform. They had some field glasses and a radio to Burnaston. I was given the glasses to hold, but couldn't hold them because they were so heavy. They used to make cups of tea in a big black shed which had an oil stove. The shed had sandbags all around it. My dad was in the Observer Corps until he joined the RAF at the beginning of 1943. He was on duty most nights.

Towards the end of the war, he was stationed at Croydon,

attached to Transport Command. He repaired the aircraft and went out to where they had come down if they had got into trouble. He'd been to Amsterdam just after it had been liberated and I, being a fussy little devil with my food, was playing up about Sunday dinner. I remember him saying, "Well the little Dutch children would eat this, their legs are as thick as your two fingers!" I never forgot that. He also told me about being in Rekyavik once where he saw the longest "Monopoly" school. It had been going for 48 hours because they were fog bound. I can remember my first banana. Two girls lived with us and one of them was going out with an American soldier based at Newton who brought the bananas. They saved me one and I took it to my mother to ask her what it was. Eventually I managed to get into it and I took one bite and spat it out. It was horrible!

We got an orange ration. My mother used to pump these oranges down me and I was allergic to them. My arms and legs had to be bandaged up to stop me scratching because I'd come out in great big rashes.

All the food stuffs were fortified with vitamins. I liked dried egg and loved tinned jam, apricot was lovely. A real treat for us was milk jelly.

Across from the Cedars on High Street there were some nurseries down between two houses. If there were any tomatoes going we'd form a huge queue and you were allowed so many. Thursday was the day you used to go with a basin to Grimley's for savoury ducks which were baked in Vaughan's across the road, where Mr Bun is now. They baked them at the bake-house and carried them across in steaming trays. We also used to go to Tom's dad, Mr Pegg's, for ice cream. You used to take your own basin. The meat from Grimley's was offal as offal wasn't rationed. Our butcher had a system where if your initial came up that week you could have something extra, a bit of suet or offal. Rabbits were always a great supplement. I remember Bill Mellors who worked for Webb's Butchers and if I was lucky he'd give me a tiny piece of beef suet for me to chew and I loved it. Can you imagine now doing that sort of thing?

Meat tended to be fatty and my mother used to boil it and then let it cool and the fat would then float on the surface. She'd use that for putting on toast and things like that. We used to put our kitchen scraps out for somebody that kept pigs. It was a crime to waste anything. If you kept pigs or fowls you were given a supplement for feed.

The anti-aircraft guns used to make a row, there were some on Osmaston Road at the bottom of Nightingale Road in Derby. I can also remember the barrage balloons. They used to cause havoc when they got loose, drifting around with their cables hanging underneath, cutting off electricity supplies all over the place.

The fellow that lived around the corner from us, Reg Cook was a Fighter Pilot based at Burnaston. He used to fly over, waggling his wings to let Cecily know he was alright. He was killed in 1948. He was flying a Lancaster that went down over the Andes. They found his body ten years later.

I was ten years old when war was declared and we were on holiday at Mablethorpe. The whole family listened to Mr Chamberlain's speech on the radio and I wondered why everybody was looking so serious. I didn't realise what war was. We came back to Castle Donington and the first strange thing I noticed was the blackout. There were no street lights and we missed the sound of church bells on Sundays as we lived on Eastway.

Castle Donington Park was requisitioned as a Vehicle Reserve Depot. The village had lots of soldiers coming in and houses were requisitioned to billet them including the Stone House, the Baptist Church Rooms etc. A forces canteen was opened at the Methodist Chapel. The cinema was open and it was always full.

In 1944 I started work at Donington Park as a trainee Civil Servant and I recall one day just before the final push into Germany, seeing troops and vehicles representing every Allied nation. At Donington Park there were also German POWs from Gopsall. By then I had gone up in the world and was working for the Colonel that commanded the Vehicle Depot. That brought me into contact with the POWs representatives. The prisoners were housed in the old ATS Camp after Gopsall Park closed.

T F Pegg

Castle Donington in the War Years

First thoughts, on that Sunday morning of 3rd September 1939, were, What happens now? for the Spanish Civil War news and reports from Poland showed how ruthlessly efficient the German forces were and, in spite of the efforts done since Munich (1938), we were far from being organised for total war.

Fortunately for us, the warfare did not turn this way at first, so we had a breathing space to try to adjust to the situation. Rationing of food and petrol were rapidly implemented, but it was the Blackout that was most difficult to cope with, and was extremely difficult and dangerous especially with car headlights being masked, and even small hand torches had black paper shrouding them (plus the fact that any torch batteries became difficult to obtain). The police

Specials, and ARP Wardens were zealous in their task to ensure the darkness was maintained. "Put that light out!" was a constant cry, not always politely put. Any strangers too were regarded with suspicion and the newly issued Identity Cards were usually asked for. The local cinema quickly adjusted to the situation, and became quite important, for in addition to ordinary films it had news items from all fronts, plus Home Front items issued by the Government.

When the war began, the Methodist Church had a fairly large group of late teenagers known as The Young Men's Class, built up over the years by Mr James Bosworth (known to us all as Jim). As they began to be called away to the Armed Forces, it was decided to keep in touch by a monthly letter, to be written by various personalities to provide variation. The letter was duplicated by Miss Mabel Chettle, then dispatched by the class secretary, who also tried to check on the addresses.

Due to my disability I was unable to join the Forces, so it eventually fell to my lot to see to this task, and I'm pleased to say that it continued to the end of hostilities. There were also Comfort Funds, run by each of the Churches, and one formed in the village which sent monetary gifts to the serving men, usually at Christmas.

Unfortunately, as the war went on, all the men of my age were called up, and it began to feel quite lonely in the village, but I became a frequent helper at the canteen. Letter writing plus first the Home Guard and then the ATC kept me quite busy. I began to collect a weekly magazine called The War Illustrated which continued throughout the war and gave a fairly good record of events as they occurred.

Army units began to arrive both in the village and at Donington Park. Church Halls and houses were requisitioned to accommodate them. The Methodist schoolrooms in the Dovecote became the dining room and social centre for the local units. The Methodist Church also opened up its Church premises as a canteen in the evenings, where the soldiers could relax and have a cup of tea and a sandwich. Occasionally, a soldier who could not read or write, would come into the canteen and ask if someone could read his mail and write a reply for him.

Later, work started on an RAF aerodrome, where the East Midlands Airport now stands, which gave added interest to me when completed, as I have always been interested in aviation matters - it also brought an influx of RAF personnel into the area.

With the early over-running of Poland, then the collapse of France in 1940, things changed drastically: First we had a lot of soldiers at the Park who were evacuated from Dunkirk for regrouping; then after the Battle of Britain (in southern skies) we had the night raids, with the German bombers seeming able to roam at will in the night skies, although the heavy bombing seemed aimed at the larger towns and ports, who had a terrible time. We had some very unpleasant nights, of course, but they seemed to have been caused by aircraft which were lost or been damaged, so we escaped with minor damage.

The Home Guard was also formed about this time, a group of willing volunteers with more enthusiasm than expertise or equipment. Their headquarters were at the Sailors and Soldiers Club in a well sand-bagged room. Mr Arthur Astle seemed to have been the man in charge and he eventually organised them into a reasonably run group, although looking back over those days, I think it was a blessing that the expected paratroopers never arrived, for by all accounts they were a ruthless lot, who neither expected nor gave any quarter. We also had a local squadron of the Air Training Corps, with other local villages, formed to provide training in aviation matters for men who eventually joined the Royal Air Force.

Due to my known interest in aviation I was asked to join as a civilian instructor, my subjects being aircraft recognition and aerodynamics, whilst others taught the rudiments of astro-navigation etc. The training also included visits to RAF Stations. Although I was a civilian instructor, I mentioned to the officers that I would also like to take part in these, so they obtained a uniform for me and by keeping in the middle of the others I was able to spend some interesting weekends, including flying, if we were lucky.

I well remember on one such visit - it was a scorching hot day - we had spent most of the day helping on an aircraft dispersal point, several of us were on our way back to the dining hall, a very untidy scruffy lot of ATC cadets we were too - tunics undone, hats tucked under shoulder straps etc. We were just passing a group of Nissen huts when a stentorian voice bellowed out at us. An RAF Warrant Officer came out, almost bursting a gasket with wrath as he came. However, when he realised he had not got pukka recruits, he smartened us up, gave us a lecture and sent us on our way, most relieved I might add.

As the Allied Air Forces began to gain supremacy over France, news began to filter through of the new air aces. Flying alongside personalities like Wing Commander Bader was a character named Johnny Johnson, who was on equal status with the best of them. He turned out to be Jimmy Johnson, who had spent his boyhood at Castle Donington and actually lived at the lower end of Borough Street when his father was the police sergeant here.

Actually I knew the family well, as there was a younger brother named Russell who was in my class at school and I spent some happy hours at their house. Jim was quite a few years older than us of course, and even then was quite a character in the village, so when recently attending a ceremony at the History Museum when a copy of a book he had written was presented to them, I was pleased to hear that he had also enquired after "the young fellow who had got himself run over by a car in Borough Street, who used to play with his brother".

The war ploughed on relentlessly and although the casualties were not as heavy as World War One, nevertheless they were school-boy friends and someone's loved ones, so the news always brought sadness to many. We were all greatly relieved when the war ended and familiar faces began to reappear back in the streets again. We were also able to listen to the sound of the church bells after they had been silent for such a long time.

I would like to conclude this account of war-time Castle Donington with the story of one of my friends, who failed to return - I have chosen *him* because perhaps I know more about his particular story, as we were such good friends. This does not detract in anyway from the achievements of the others who also gave their all for us and their country.

Bill Massey and I began school together at the tender age of four and usually shared the same desk in class. Our mothers were good friends too. I can picture them still, watching proudly as we advanced through school, often taking parts in the various plays and pageants that Miss Chell, the Junior School headmistress, was so good at organising. I heard my first wireless set at their house. Our ways parted for a while when Bill succeeded in passing the eleven plus exams, (the only one in our year to achieve a full pass) so off he went to Loughborough College (the Tec as we knew it!) whilst the rest of us proceeded through the usual village education. When I left school to start work in the town of Loughborough, we usually travelled on the same bus, and renewed our friendship again. He was an unpretentious lad, who loved our village and its traditions. He helped to form the local Scout group, also the local unit of the Air Training Corps during the war years.

Eventually he volunteered for the RAF and was accepted for flying crew. I must admit I was more than a little envious when he went but, when he came home on leave, we had many chats together. He trained as a navigator/observer and had almost completed his training when the plane he was flying in crashed, killing all of the crew. He was buried in the local cemetery with a military funeral and full honours including a volley of rifle shots as he was buried. In addition to the RAF squad, the local ATC formed a Guard of Honour and acted as coffin bearers. It was a very sad day for us as he was lowered into the ground - at his mother's request I formed part of the ATC Guard of Honour. I have not chosen Bill for any other reason than that he was a very good friend. I have included him, as he would have wished, as a typical Donington lad of our age, who did his duty as he saw it.

This is my own tribute to all of the chaps who did not return and who really need no Armistice Ceremony to recall the happy moments shared - although it does help us as a reminder of the passing years.

Arthur Smith (Smudge)

The son of George Edward Smith was called Smudge. Arthur Smith, reputed to be the finest plasterer in the Midlands, called Smudge after his Dad, was forced to go down the pit. He was sixteen when the war broke out and was working in the building trade but as the war continued work got tight and he was forced to to look for another job. He got a job at Nailstone Colliery on the surface. When he was eighteen he went to enlist in the Forces; the Navy being his first choice. He was rejected because he was working at the pit. He applied six more times for the Forces including the "Paras" and to be a rear gunner in the R.A.F. He was told he must go down the pit. With a few more pals he refused and was eventually summonsed. He was fined six pounds ten shillings or a month in jail. His father and himself had the money to pay the fine but he refused thinking that after spending a month in jail he would then be free to enter the Forces. He was wrong. He went to jail but while in there his fine was paid and he was let out. He paid his fine money to the persons who had paid it. The fine had gone up to six pounds twelve shillings. Two shillings went to the jail for keeping him.

His case was a test trial for the country. He had bucked the government and lost. Funnily, just after his ordeal, they brought the Bevin Boy Scheme out. So young Smudge finished up down the pit for the duration of the war.

F H W Moore

My Part In The Destruction Of Nazi Germany

I was nearing sixteen years of age and working at Herbert Morris Ltd, the Loughborough crane builders, on that Friday morning, September 1st, 1939. We were setting a crab frame up for the welder, Mr Harper, at about 11.30 am, when suddenly another workman rushed in to the cubicle with a copy of the Leicester Mercury special edition, bearing the banner headline "Germany Invades Poland - War Imminent". Of course this news had an un-nerving effect initially but, within a matter of weeks, war fever took over. The sinking of the SS Athenia, coupled with government propaganda imploring everybody to "Do their bit" for the war effort, soon brought out the adventurous spirit of Britain's youth. Long queues were soon to be seen outside recruiting offices throughout the length and breadth of the land.

We all listened to Chamberlain's speech at 11 am, Sunday 3rd September, in which he stated that as Herr Hitler had not complied with the British and French ultimatum demanding the withdrawal of German forces from Poland, a state of war would exist between Britain and Germany.

Of course, being too young to join up, also under the conscription age limit, we were soon to find ourselves in reserved occupations, under the governments "Essential Works Order".

And so we found ourselves in a state of fear of the unknown. My friends and I went to the Saturday night "flicks" as usual. The Grand was showing a film "Suez" starring Annabell. At the declaration of war, the next day, all public places of entertainment were closed to reduce the risk of mass casualties from air raids. The government relaxed this measure after a couple of weeks for cinemas and theatres with adequate emergency exits. The Grand apparently did not have these and was eventually commandeered to become a "buffer" store. Another blow to the district's younger population was the immediate closure of the Public Baths in Avenue Road. These were to become a casualty clearing station and a civil defence depot for the duration. I was working in Loughborough at this time, and I remember some of the rumours that were circulated during those early months. One day it was said that German parachutists had landed in Charnwood Forest and were trying to contact certain people in town. Of course, to those of us who were cycling the ten miles daily to work, this became a matter of grave concern. However we timorously cycled our way back home, negotiating Nanpantan, Charley and Copt Oak without sighting a single Hun.

We very soon found ourselves buried at work. The Essential Works Order was introduced, and although not yet sixteen years old, we were required to work two hours overtime at night, and until four o'clock in the afternoon on Saturdays and Sundays. 1939-40 was a nasty year for me. I suffered two bouts of tonsillitis, and was sent to the Leicester Royal Infirmary to have them removed. This illness, like many others, was a serious business, there being no antibiotics at that time. I had to go to the Infirmary on a Wednesday, 29th May 1940, and the wards were filling up with wounded soldiers from Belgium and France, and what a time the less seriously wounded gave those over-worked nurses.

In the latter part of 1939, before food rationing was introduced, the well-to-do were buying up and stock-piling as much non-perishable and canned food-stuffs as they could. Conscription was introduced, and week by week familiar friends would disappear from the local scene as they were called up for service in the forces, sadly, many of them never to return, giving all for King and Country. Mid December brought a surge of expectancy, when the three British destroyers took on the mighty German battleship Graf Spee. These pocket battleships were causing great distress to the British convoys in the Atlantic Ocean, sinking boats carrying vital supplies of food and war materials from the USA. The three ships, Achilles, Exeter and Ajax, forced the Graf Spee into Montevideo harbour for battle damage repairs, but the harbour authorities refused permission, and she was scuttled.

26th January 1940 saw the start of the worst blizzard within living memory. It started on a Friday and didn't stop until Tuesday. Gritting of roads was yet to be introduced, as in 1940 the railways were still the major transport system. Buses were unable to take the workers to mines and factories. When it eventually stopped, I walked to Coalville to catch the Loughborough bus, but only got as far as Gracedieu ruins. Some workmen tried to get through on foot, and some of them eventually did. I and some others tried one morning but as we ascended the hill past the Gracedieu Manor, it was a passageway for one person only, through drifts six to ten foot high, and became too frightening for us to continue. After a week there was another fall of snow, but fortunately, although heavy, it was sporadic, and lasted only two days.

January 1940 saw everyone issued with a ration book. Tea, sugar, meat, cream, butter and petrol were soon in short supply and many other food products went "under the counter" to be available only to the better class people. By mid 1940 large queues were forming outside the large multiple food stores.

I left Herbert Morris's at the end of August 1940 and started working for Pegsons at Coalville, where eventually I became apprenticed. At about this time, I went with a friend to see the Home Guard practising at the Ellistown Colliery. The Home Guard was originally the Local Defence Volunteers, formed by the government at the time of Dunkirk, as an added defence against parachutists and saboteurs. We were soon inveigled into joining by shouts of "Come and join us" by those parading in their denims and shouldering wooden rifles. I was too young to be officially enrolled, but because I had a good bicycle, I was taken on as a "runner".

The first air raid warning in the Coalville district was sounded on 24th June 1940. The sirens sounded the warning at 12.30 am and the all-clear was given at 4 am. Air raids were every night from June 1940 until the turn of the tide about the time of El Alamein. Coalville, being in the flight path of one of Hitler's prime targets, the Rolls Royce plant at Derby, ensured plenty of passing enemy aircraft overhead. Occasionally, I would be walking from Coalville when the many searchlight detachments would suddenly turn night into day with the many beams probing the sky in search of the raiders, so as to provide the ack-ack gunners with an easy target. I remember one such night, as we watched the searching beams of light, an enemy plane was caught, and he immediately circled round and flew down the beam with his guns blazing. The light was extinguished, and within a day or two we heard that several soldiers had been killed by this action at the Altons searchlight unit on the road to Ashby.

Although not being old enough to imbibe myself, I well remember the beer shortage, which began around June 1941. Cigarettes had been in short supply for some time. Although Pasha, Nosegay and Abdullah were readily available, we used to rap on the off-sales window of the "snugs" and try to buy a pack of a better known brand.

As an apprentice at Pegsons, if you were not on production work, you were required to do plane spotting on the night shift. To perform this task, we had to take our place in the water tower. This was a structure, sixty foot high with a 40,000 gallon water tank on top, which had in its centre a glass observation compartment. This building, now demolished, was the original winding house for Stephenson's No 1 Snibstone colliery. The foresight of this great man matched his other achievements inasmuch as this observation point, constructed over one hundred years previously, was custom built for the purpose.

I remember when the heavy bombing raids started, we had a mother and baby from Birmingham billeted with us. They stayed some twelve weeks, and I remember her husband coming one Sunday and telling her she had got to return home as the bombing raids had diminished greatly.

I suppose the highlight of my war was a trip to London on 31st October 1942 with my father, to hear Winston Churchill address the miners in the Central Hall, Westminster. Three thousand delegates from all over Britain were present, representing managememt and men. Coal production was flagging and Churchill had the idea that a grand occasion would help raise the extra tons of coal. Well, a grand occasion it really was, with all the members of the War Cabinet present, the Massed Bands of Guards and the BBC's Sandy MacPherson at the organ. Field Marshall Smuts of South Africa was the guest speaker. Churchill ended his speech with the words"... and someday when your children ask "What did you do Daddy to win this great inheritance for us?" One will say - I flew a Spitfire during the Battle of Britain - another will say - I braved the Nazi wolf packs in the Atlantic Ocean - a third will say - I marched with Montgomery at El Alamein, but you in your turn will say with equal right and with equal pride - "I CUT THE COAL". The miners, many of whom had detested this man from the 1926 era, gave him a lengthy standing ovation.

I remember we had a letter of thanks from Field Marshall Montgomery for our efforts in producing the six-pounder anti-tank gun. This was displayed on the factory notice board. We produced rammers for the forces engineers, two inch pumps for the invasion barges, and just prior to the invasion itself, we produced many thousand links which had everybody guessing whatever part of the war effort could they be. Of course, after the invasion, it became known they were part of the top-secret Mulberry Harbour.

Coalville Co-op Bakery baked bread for the blitzed Midland cities and as we went to work in the morning the vans were seen loading up in Baker Street.

In the spring of 1940, I was cycling back from a visit to the cinema, when I was stopped by the police for having a bright light on my bicycle. I was subsequently summoned to appear at the Coalville Magistrates' Court, where the case against me was dismissed on the payment of four shillings costs. The sitting magistrate was a Mr J West, a printer, who due to a hearing impediment, used an ear trumpet.

August 28th was the night the Germans bombed Coalville. At about 10.30 pm a plane, no doubt returning after a fruitless attempt to penetrate Derby's anti-aircraft defences, decided to jettison his bombs rather than take them back to his homeland. The bombs, about eight, struck a house in London Road, Granville Villas, against Robinson's Morris garage, causing damage to the roof and gable end brickwork. There were no casualties.

A German Messerschmidt 109 fighter plane which had made a forced landing in the South of England, was put on show throughout the country, and was on Victoria Park, Leicester in August 1940. It later came to Coalville and was on display to the rear of the Constitutional Club, where the precinct now stands.

October 30th 1940 saw bombs dropped at Hugglescote, damaging some fowl pens, causing the hens to lay a few blood-shot eggs, but no civilian casualties.

On November 14th 1940, Coventry was practically destroyed in an all night raid by the Luftwaffe. A party of us from work cycled over on the Sunday afternoon to view the damage. Parts of the city centre were roped off, obviously for safety reasons, and all the undamaged cinemas and halls were opened as temporary shelter for those made homeless.

On the 19th and 20th of November 1940, Leicester City suffered its worst air attack of the war. Freeman Hardy & Willis and Faire Bros were the two largest factories to be gutted by the bombers, much more damage being caused to other properties, including civilian homes. This raid destroyed the needle plant of T Grieve & Co in Queen Street, which after the war was resited in the vacant Wolsey factory in Coalville.

During the war years the Ministry of Information regularly put on film shows in local venues and factory canteens. They also had talks by shipwrecked sailors and battle scarred warriors, all in an attempt to keep our morale up. I well remember the ENSA shows put on for the war workers. Some of the shows were quite good, but most lived up to the alternative version of their acronym - Every Night Something Awful.

As the war years passed, I remember the introduction of PAYE in 1944. As the war contracts started to dry up, there were big schemes set up to recruit men for the mines (Bevin Boys) and scores were drafted into the armed forces to fill the vacuum created by de-mobilisation of wartime conscripts.

Ensor Johnson

My son was born six weeks after I went into the forces. I had a telegram to say he had been born at the Nightingale Maternity Home in Derby and so I asked for compassionate leave and was told, "You're in the army now. You're not getting any compassionate leave." I was in Lincoln barracks and I decided to come without leave. Everywhere was alive with Red Caps - Military Police. It was the 21st Army Group and people were deserting. I went to Derby Station from Lincoln dodging the Red Caps and got to the Nightingale where the matron told me that I was going to be disappointed because my wife and son had both been very ill and were fast asleep and couldn't be disturbed. "You'll have to come back after dinner and then you'll be allowed ten minutes," she said.

I went outside and there were Red Caps who would have arrested me immediately, so I set off for Castle Donington. A few people passed me in cars but nobody picked me up so I walked to Donington and went up to my mother-in-law's where she cooked me a dinner. I started back to Derby and the Nightingale and someone picked me up. At the Nightingale I was let in and saw my wife and son, Stuart, for ten minutes or so. Afterwards, I got back to the station and then on to Lincoln without being caught. Chaps that I knew had stood in and covered for me. They never knew that I had gone!

Margaret Lindner

I was born Margaret Cook in July 1935, so really my earliest memory was of going to the Church School on Castle Hill, Castle Donington, where the Catholic Church is now. The most important thing was to carry your gas mask. When it was raining my mum used to make me carry it under my coat so I looked like the Hunchback of Notre Dame going to school and I was ribbed about that. We had gas drill where we'd don our gas masks and troop down to the cloakroom and just sit on oval rush mats until such time as they decided we knew the drill.

We lived on Bond Gate and I remember seeing plenty of army convoys, quite a lot of soldiers and once, a bus with a huge gas bag on the top. We thought it was great fun. I don't remember any of the horror of war. To we children is was all a big game. We were cushioned against the horror of it. Nevertheless, we played our part by taking sixpences for National Savings Stamps. We saved silver paper and took it to the Post Office on Borough Street. We gathered rose hips in the autumn and took them to the chemist for making into rose hip syrup which was a rich source of vitamin C. We never wasted anything. We were the original recyclers. There were quite a number of properties that lost their iron railings and they collected pots and pans for the war effort. We ate everything that was put in front of us because we were always hungry. There is one thing I can't stand now and that is bread and scrape. It wasn't butter. Whatever you had to scrape was put on bread and we were always made to eat at least some of it.

My dad used to smoke thick twist. It was foul and used to smoke everybody out of the house. Sometimes, if he was a bit short of tobacco, he would shred it up and suck on it. I've known him put dried tea leaves in his pipe and smoke that. He dug up the front garden to grow vegetables and grew tomatoes up the south-facing wall at the front.

I don't remember anything pre-war so rationing and shortages were natural for us. We used to queue up to spend our sweet ration and then dash off to the cinema for the weekly matinee to see Roy Rogers etc. We had a lot of freedom and could play anywhere in Castle Donington.

We did have an air raid when we lived on Bond Gate. We had a cellar and if there was an air raid warning, we were scurried off down the cellar steps. On this particular night several bombs were dropped. The raid went on all night and when we went back into the kitchen, the next morning, there was a terrible mess. There was soot and broken glass everywhere and the blackout curtain was in shreds. When we went outside we saw that the telegraph wires in Bond Gate were down. Our house was on the corner and it had taken the brunt of the blast. It was as if the house had been lifted up and plonked back down again. We were very excited, running around trying to find bits of shrapnel. We had to have the back of the house rebuilt as it was unsafe. I think that there was only one casualty that night. A cow was killed.

A friend of mine who lived in a house with no garden had a Morrison shelter in their large living room. We loved playing in that as it was like a big den. We had many happy hours in that shelter.

Windmill Fields, where I now live, was all fields then and the aerodrome was up there. I remember a plane coming down at the end of the runway near the top of High Street. I don't know if anyone was killed but I do remember it going off the runway.

My father was wounded in the First World War, he lost an eye, so he was not called up. I don't know whether he was an official ARP but he always seemed to be out during air raids. He would go round looking for chinks of light and if any light showed the people responsible got a warning and then a fine, if it continued. We used to wear white badges that glowed in the dark when we went out at night and had to have identity cards.

We never went on holiday. A holiday for us was to go to Alveston Park where there was a paddling pool. In the school holidays we used to troop down to paddle in Hemington brook with jam sandwiches and a bottle of water. We weren't very sophisticated but we had a good time and it didn't cost anything.

I was in South Shields at the end of the war. My sister had married and I was staying with her parents-in-law. I went to school there for one or two weeks and they had street parties all over the estate where we were staying. I remember it being a great time. Everybody was very happy.

Bruce Townsend

My father was a Sergeant in the Home Guard in Holbrook. He was about sixty then, so it was quite strenuous for him. At the start of the war their arms were limited to broomsticks and things like that to practise drill with. Eventually, they were issued with one rifle and five rounds of ammunition, and they took it in turns to patrol the village at night.

It was the turn of the farmer to patrol his own land when suddenly he saw a poacher. The village policeman! He'd had a lot of trouble with poachers and with the village policeman who was a cantankerous swine who I remember well. The policeman had been harrassing the farmer and there was no love lost between them, so when he spotted the policeman poaching, he fired a shot through some trees above his head. He didn't shoot to kill, I think he would have liked to. This caused my father a lot of worry as he had to explain, to his superiors, as to how a round of ammunition had disappeared.

David G Devante Pownall

On March 18th, 1943 I joined the army in Leicester and had my initial primary training at the Leicester Race Course, billeted in the stables with three other Officer Training Cadets. After six weeks we were posted to whatever regiment we preferred. My preference was the Royal Army Ordnance Corps and so I was posted to Oxford where I received advanced training in Armoured "A" and "B" vehicles. I became interested in motor cycles, BSA, Nortons, Matchless, Ariels, AJS, etc., so I volunteered to become a dispatch rider taking a course in Nuneaton. By April 1944 and prior to the Normandy landings, I was posted to Charnwood Forest and billeted in the farmhouse adjacent to the Belfry and in close proximity to the Monastery. It was there I took my first dreaded but exciting CARDA course which meant intensive and dangerous infantry training. This training included hand to hand fighting to simulate the real thing as if in battle. We used firearms with live ammunition such as Bren Guns, automatic Sten Guns fired from the shoulder and waist, also the 303 Rifle sometimes with fixed bayonets. The most frightening experience was priming a 36 Mills hand grenade and actually throwing them live. If they failed to detonate we were ordered to creep up to the spot in order that to defuse and reprime or hurl them at the next target.

The rifle range with its stout red brick compound is still standing to this day in the field of the farmhouse facing the Belfry and can clearly be seen from the road. Nature and I suspect the present owners have been kind because it still it looks almost in as good a condition as it was fifty years ago. There are a few nettles and brambles which have taken root but it can easily be recognised as a wartime rifle range with its buttresses all intact.

I often visit the Forest near to the range. It never fails to attract me and I have to look in that direction. Its like a magnet to me. My memories are vividly clear and constantly re-lived: The gaunt menacing dummy German-helmeted Wermacht Hun stuffed with hay, and in the centre of this formidable row there was just one with black hair hanging over its right eye to one side with a small moustache. It had been repeatedly thrust deeply through its body with fixed bayonets and become so mutilated it no longer resembled Hitler. We were taught to hate the Hun. During those few brief moments, as I slowly drive by, the past haunts me. No one knows the torment I go through. I feel at times so sad that I might be the only one left to remember those exciting days. As a young platoon leader and cadet I knew every rock and hillock as far as the Forest Rock and Quarry. We fought as if for real, not knowing it would be for real within a few weeks time in Normandy. Even now whenever I see the old farmhouse, the rifle range, the rocks and hills I have to suppress my overwhelming emotions. It brings a lump to my throat and I ask myself am I the only one left to remember the range?

Anonymous

Someone Else's Thunder.

I was one of the original militia, those nineteen year olds who were registered for the forces early in 1939 and grabbed just before or just after the war broke out. I was grabbed just after.

Three months' basic training on the cold east coast of Scotland changed us from civilians into super-fit young soldiers and then a number of us were sent to Oxford for specialised Corps training. This completed, we were kitted out ready to go to Norway but the campaign there collapsed before we reached it.

In the meantime the Army had learned something of the new warfare, particularly about strafing of troop columns by aircraft, so it was decided we should learn to cope with that before we moved on. We were taken out into the country, carrying full kit, and a light plane from a nearby RAF station made passes over us from all angles.

He was a good pilot and a crafty so-and-so. We marched along listening and watching for him swooping in on us, when we had to dive into any ditch or cover we could reach before he came overhead. He arrived from all angles, taking advantage of every hill or stand of wood to surprise us. By the time evening came it was no longer a game. We were tired, dirty and completely fed up.

So we were a bedraggled lot as we made our way back to our billets, across Magdalen Bridge and along the High. It was around five o'clock and the streets were busy with people going home from work. Suddenly we realised that they had stopped walking home, and were lining up on the pavements, smiling at us and applauding as we passed.

Our heads came up, our pride was restored and we marched back like bantam cocks. It wasn't until we reached our billets and tuned in our wireless sets we learned that day, 27th May, 1940, was the start of the evacuation from Dunkirk and that the good people of Oxford had mistaken us for war-weary troops returning from the beaches.

As a footnote, a couple of weeks later we issued with tropical kit and warned of the dire fate that could befall our ship if we told anyone we were going East and the news reached the U-boats. The warning was repeated at every parade, then came the day we had to entrain for port. Again we marched through the busy streets of Oxford, none of us having dared even hint where we were going, again in full kit, but this time with our pith helmets carefully strapped in the middle of our back pack!

Ex-Bombardier Taylor L F

Called up to the Royal Artillery Barracks at Oswestry in 1940, I was "put through the hoops" for two months' basic training and then on to Towyn Royal Artillery Firing Camp for another month's "fun", firing heavy shells at aircraft. It *was* quite good fun too - they did not fire back.

Training completed, we were given seven days' leave which, in my case, was occupied by chasing around for a special licence to marry my fiancee. After the ceremony, at Ibstock church, on Wednesday, and a very short honeymoon at home, I headed back to Towyn on Saturday. One big regret, over the next 54 years was that, due to an acute shortage of photographic materials, there were no wedding photographs.

Whilst changing stations at Birmingham, on the return journey to Towyn, shouts from newspaper sellers told me that London was suffering its first daytime bombing raid. The effect of this news was soon to affect me as, arriving at Towyn at midnight we were not even allowed off the train, instead our kit, already packed for us, was coupled to our train and off we went to the capital.

Arriving at a gun-site on the outskirts of London early on Sunday morning, we were in action by that afternoon as three Stuka bombers screamed down to attack the factories we were there to protect. This was to be, for me, the start of a long and often exciting war. Belonging to the First Division Anti-Aircraft Division our task was the defence of the capital. We saw lots of action in and around London at many different gun-sites, first against daytime and then night-time raids. Needless to say I grabbed every opportunity, official and sometimes unofficial, to get home for a decent night's sleep with, of course, the added attraction of my new bride. After two years defending London our next orders took us the length and breadth of Great Britain in convoy, travelling to battle schools for special training for the forthcoming invasion. It was tough, hard work, worse, in many ways than the bombing.

Next came the heady days preparing for D-Day. There was a real buzz to know that, at last, we were having a go at "Jerry", instead of all the defending we were "in the driving seat". It came as an anti-climax when, after waterproofing the big guns for the hazardous channel crossing, we were suddenly pulled back, ordered to de-waterproof and travel to the south east coast. Hitler's latest hi-tech weapon, the flying bomb, was the reason for our change of orders. At first they were very daunting but soon we were to have great fun shooting them out of the skies.

Eventually, when a new line of artillery was established down to the South-East coast, we were released for the Normandy Invasion. We were loaned to the American army and landed, with them, at Utah beach-head. After making out way to Cherbourg we were assigned cliff-top positions and took on the multi-roles of anti-aircraft, coastal protection, anti-tank and generally covering all possible strikes the Germans might make. Losses in that time were very light and at the out-set of the push through Caen and the Falaise gap, we were pulled back to the British sector and headed for Belgium. On reaching Brussels we set up as defence against air attacks on that city but as things were relatively quiet, we were allowed a little R & R in that capital.

As the first soldiers into the city, there being no Belgian francs available, we were given special "funny money" to spend. When I offered to settle the bill at the Au'Ballon Cafe the waiter refused to accept it but after calling for the manager the matter was resolved without us having to wash the pots or even fighting our way out.

A couple sitting watching the action asked to see this new money, so I gave him a small note as a souvenir. We struck up a friendship that has lasted over fifty years, writing two or three times a year with occasional visits which, of course, bring us out in fits of nostalgia but also makes us realise how lucky we are to have come safely through those desperate times.

Fighting our way into Holland and then back again to Belgium during the Battle of the Bulge, we eventually went into Germany. Sent to Hamburg, we were given the job of sorting out German POWs, many were shipped up into Denmark. Another big headache were the many displaced persons who often had to be guarded for their own good. At this time we were forbidden to talk to any Germans by a Non-fraternization ban. I still have one of the original Orders of the Day announcing the ban.

Having settled the war in Europe we began to train for a very different war, in the Far East, and hopefully bring an early finish there. Thankfully, and I use that word advisedly, that was brought to an abrupt end by the two Atom Bombs. Although most people condemn the carnage caused by these bombs, I must stress the Japanese were the aggressors and it saved many allied lives.

I stayed in Hamburg for a year until I was demobbed in May 1946. Six years of my life had been totally disrupted. I had two sons who did not know me and who I hardly knew. I had slept rough for the whole six years so it took a long time to settle back into Civvy Street, in fact a whole year.

The positive thing that came out of the conflict was the great comradeship and for people, particularly service people, that comradeship has stood the test of time. It certainly taught people to pull together for better times. I only hope it does not take another war to pull everyone together again.

I have enjoyed writing and re-living the "better" memories of war time.

W. D. Maltby

Kegworth youngster during the war

During the bombing raids by the Germans in the early Forties, two primary targets in the Midlands were Coventry and the Rolls Royce factories at Derby, (for whom, incidentally, the local Slack & Parr factory machined components). Those of us who had no Anderson shelter converted the pantry or "glory-hole" under the stairs as a refuge, it being evident from war photographs that in the event of being hit, this area was usually the part of the house left standing. I spent many nights thus ensconced, hearing Gerry droning above the pounding of heavy naval Ack-Ack guns defending Derby. (One could always tell a German plane by its distinctive "hum-hum-hum").

One night however, we were fooled! We were all in bed having no warning siren, when suddenly we heard a lone plane. Obviously one of a formation which had got lost, for I heard this drone over, and although my first instinct was that it was a German, since it did pass over, and there was no responding flak, I concluded that for once I was mistaken, and that it was one of ours lost whilst returning from an offensive mission. A little while later and he returned going the other way, and again, - no flak. When yet later it commenced to pass over for the third time, I was by now quite blasè. Folly!! We were all lulled into a false sense of security. All of a sudden I heard whistling. I have never got out of bed so fast! Before the bomb had landed I had cleared all thirteen stairs, crossed the dining room, and was in the pantry, - in time to hear an almighty bang and feel the house shake. My father, who had been outside on "fire-watch" duty had also reached the pantry, and we both thought, that's in our back garden!

The following day we discovered, however, that a land mine had landed at Kingston-on-Soar. Fortunately for that small community it had missed the hard surface of the road and landed in a field, leaving a huge crater and killing a few hens. A split second's release earlier or later and the entire village would have been blown off the map. Hard luck on the hens, but that bomb was an expensive investment for Adolf!

V. M. Dolman

Jerry pays a visit to Snibston Lodge Farm

It was a very light, moonlit night and the drone of German aircraft flying overhead in the early hours of Good Friday morning, 1941, kept us awake. Several times I sat on the bottom of my bed, looking out of the window, trying to catch sight of one of the bombers as it passed over, probably on its way to bomb Coventry. Eventually, I grew tired of jumping in and out of bed and decided to settle down for the night, but not for long, for suddenly there was the broad shrill whistle of a bomb descending followed by a loud explosion and the crashing of falling glass. Once more, I was at the bottom of my bed looking out of the window, this time, to see a large cloud of debris falling to the earth in the field at the front of our house. Two bombs had been off-loaded. Fortunately, there was no serious damage done, either to property or animals but there was not one pane of glass left whole in the windows of the house and buildings. One piece of shrapnel went through the garden wall leaving a gaping hole, another piece almost severed an electricity pole nearby. The blast even wrenched the hasps from some of the doors to the cowsheds. We certainly didn't get much sleep that night. There was a constant stream of people passing through the farm that Easter weekend to see the bomb damage.

What Jerry didn't succeed in doing that night at Snibston Lodge Farm, the National Coal Board achieved thirty-seven years later when the lovely Victorian farmhouse and buildings were razed to the ground. Snibston Grange, nearby, another handsome residence had also suffered the same fate two years previously. A large part of the farmland, as it was then, is now part of the Snibston Discovery Park.

Mrs Daisy Rodgers nee Warren

Just One Memory Of Many

My story began on the morning that Rolls Royce Derby was bombed. It is one of my most vivid memories of the war. I was a land girl at the time, attached to the

Leicestershire Section of the Land Army, headquarters at Granby Street, Leicester.

I had been directed to work for a market gardener and his father, Mr George Powdrill, whose premises were just over the Station Bridge running over the railway lines on Hemington Lane, Hemington.

It was just about 7.30 am on the Monday morning and as I cycled through the village, I passed a young lady going toward the houses on the Main Street. I learned afterwards that she had been going with her boyfriend to catch a bus to Rolls Royce at Derby where they both worked. On the way to the bus, she had felt unwell and her boyfriend advised her to return to his home where she had spent the weekend. He carried on and caught the usual bus to work.

Just after passing the young lady I became aware of the dull drone of an aircraft, very heavy and very close. The thought came to me that it was a bomber and sounded funny. As I got halfway up the bridge, this was confirmed for me when a grey plane just skimmed the top of the parapet, passing directly in front of me. The Swastika markings, the pilot and one other crew member were quite visible, the look on their faces as startled as mine. I watched them, and clearly they were following the railway lines through to Derby. I had heard of planes flying low to get under the barrage balloons ack ack fire.

I managed to get to the gate, where Mr Powdrill and his father were waiting for me, they had been watching from near the house, Old George said, "Are you alright, lass? You are the luckiest girl alive. I wish I'd got my gun, I couldn't have missed at that height. I'd have had a pop at him, he's a ruddy jerry, didn't you know?" That is when the reaction set in. We were just going into the house when the sirens sounded and straight away the sound of the bombs. They'd hit their target Rolls Royce, killing quite a few workers and injuring more.(sadly the young man from Hemington was among the dead). Did that young girl have a premonition? I've often wondered.

Quite a few Castle Donington people who worked there were treated for shock and injuries and many were sent home. I was also told to go home for the day. Mr Powdrill said he didn't think I could do much after that.

A Highton

Long Whatton during the War Years

Long Whatton like many other villages was geared up for any situation that may arise. Being in a somewhat safe zone we had evacuees from London as well as a maternity home at Whatton House where many babies were born. Some who didn't survive were laid to rest in the village church yard. This last few years we have met many people finding Whatton House to see where they were born.

We had a company of Home Guard as well as Civil Defence personnel. The Methodist Chapel was a first aid centre, fortunately never needed. In charge of this was my father George Stanley, along with my mother and Mrs Sally Lester all members of the St John's Ambulance. Air Raid Wardens patrolled the village making sure that no lights were visible. Being on the flight path for Coventry and Birmingham we could see the searchlights and guns firing, trying to fetch the planes down. Many was the time when we went over the fields in the dark to reach the first aid post.

I remember one night my father was standing at the back door of our house and a bomb was dropped. The force of the blast threw him from side to side so it was time to move. The place where it was dropped was Brook House which had previously been the Rectory, and was owned by Lord Crawshaw. The house had been rented to Lord Leverhume of Port Sunlight. The family was not at home, but a housemaid was there. Runners were dispatched to keep listening for more aircraft while the rescue party searched for the missing housemaid. The rescue party working without lights eventually found her dead on a sofa amongst the rubble.

Whatton House Park was also a target for incendiary bombs which would light up the area. Farm hands and estate workers were always on hand to deal with them. What always amazed me was that during a full moon the fields of ripe corn ready to harvest were never destroyed by fire bombs.

Between 1939 and 1942 I worked in Loughborough and you never knew what you might find the next morning and often you didn't get out of town before the sirens went which meant a ride home in the dark. In July 1942 I joined the Land Army instead of going into a munitions factory or joining the forces. This is a decision I never regretted.

We lost quite a few village boys, one being my brother-in-law, at rest in Rangie Cemetery, Singapore and from a friend's visit we now have photographs of his grave.

J. Hair

The place: New Street, Seals Road, Hill Street, Donisthorpe.

The time: August 3rd 1942 1.58 pm. Bank Holiday Monday.

The Caves Arms Public House was full of miners on their day off work, singing at the top of their voices. Old John Farmer was playing the piano. He played at all the local pubs. School children were playing in the bushes at the entrance to New Street. Suddenly a lone plane appeared in the sky with what seemed like smoke coming from it. As the children watched the cry went up, "It's a German. He's dropping bombs!"

One bomb landed in the field at the bottom of Seals Road and made a large crater. Another bomb exploded in Seals Road and some houses were eventually demolished. A man, Mr. Reynolds, died as a result of this bomb exploding.

Another bomb landed on the road outside of the Caves Arms, skidded over the public house and exploded on the pit premises. The pub was full of miners singing away. The name of the song - Bless this House! The time,1.58 pm, was the time at which the shop clock stopped when the bombs exploded.

Stretton-En-Le-Field:

During the war the Hall next to the church housed Scottish soldiers. Some of these were manning a searchlight at Willesley one night when a German plane came down the beam of the light and killed the soldiers. After the soldiers had been moved from Stretton, German prisoners of war were housed there. These men were taken out daily to work on the local farms.

Italian prisoners were held at Shellbrook, near Ashby. They were allowed to cycle to work on the farms, each of them wearing a brown boiler suit with a red circle printed on the back of the suit for identification.

Heather Chandler

Summer Afternoon

"Uncle" and I leapt to the semi-circle of the bay window. We had been working on a very large and almost totally absorbing jigsaw puzzle, but the sounds of gunfire became so loud that we felt sure there must be another dog-fight going on right overhead. It was 1940 in the midst of the Battle of Britain.

Dog-fights, that is close combat between German fighter planes and our own Spitfires, had become a frequent sight above the normally quiet countryside of mid-Surrey. We lived beneath the air route used by the bombers who were making regular attacks on London at that time, and the Spitfires sent up to thwart their purpose, were frequently engaged in fights to the death with the escort of German fighter planes. Usually we would look up to see a silent display of aerobatic flying, spectacularly performed by two dots high in the summer sky - too high to detect easily which was the enemy and which our gallant RAF. It was, however, such a fascinating test of the skill for both pilots that we applauded from below as they twisted, rolled and snaked across the sky, playing hide and seek in a cloud or winking like diamonds as they turned suddenly to catch the sunlight. Occasionally the planes would swoop so low overhead that we could identify the markings, and then it was the swastikas which attracted the attention of the nearby Ack-Ack battery dug into the local golf course.

This time we could hear the guns and knew the enemy must have come within range. It was a bit like cheering on your team in a football match. We jumped to the window to see if anything was in view. It was - a German bomber swooping towards us head on!

The house, to which I had been evacuated some months before, was situated on the edge of a small market town with a long narrow field opposite, which sloped gently down towards the East/West railway line. To the right, and only just out of our line of sight, was another railway route, the link from London to the South Coast. Thus a very important junction lay right on our doorstep.

The German bomber, which had been turned back from a daylight raid on London, was still pregnant with a belly full of bombs. Damaged by our fighters and guns, and dragged down by the death-delivering payload, the pilot must have realised that getting back across the Channel would be a problem. Lightening the load by dropping it on some other unintentioned, but so obviously important, target must have seemed an excellent solution as, flying low, he would have seen the criss-cross of railway lines directly ahead.

For a dreadful moment time seemed to stand still, imprinting that sight in my mind for ever. The plane, like a great spread-winged eagle poised in our view as if it were a picture painted within the frame of the window.

"Uncle" threw me to the floor. We waited for the explosion. The plane roared over the roof-top and there were a series of dull thuds as the stick of three bombs went off. The first fell into the soft earth at the far side of the railway embankment in a controlled explosion which left little to show afterwards; the second, too, fell into soft newly-ploughed soil in the segment of land just off the junction, and the third landed harmlessly in a water meadow just beyond. Thank goodness, in his panic, the pilot had misjudged his moment and all was safe. No damage had been done to life or the vital link-lines of the railway used regularly for troop and munitions movements. Only the scars to our local landscape remained as a point of interest on our Sunday afternoon walks.

We returned to the jigsaw. I don't think it occurred to either of us that we were probably lucky to be alive.

Kenneth M Butcher

Memories from World War Two

In 1941 a visitor informed us that a child from London was to be billeted at our house. Being ten years old and an only child, this was welcome news. David also brought his mother, who worked at an RAF rehabilitation unit.

David's father was a policeman and remained in London but was able to visit once a month to see his wife and son. On these visits he related vivid stories of narrow escapes and horrific damage. During one visit he casually asked if we would care to both receive the gift of an unexploded incendiary bomb. We didn't require a second invitation!

On the next visit, two bombs duly appeared. Some eighteen inches long with grey/green fins - otherwise they were made of pure magnesium. At the bottom end, the cap had much German writing and unscrewed with many turns. We were informed that it was safe as long as we didn't light a fire underneath!

Apparently one bomb had landed safely in a sand pit with the other having come through a damaged open roof and slid into a bath of water. You can imagine the pride with which we took our "treasures" to school at the first opportunity. Heroes for a day!

In due course the bombing in London subsided and so David and his mother returned home, plus one incendiary bomb.

Later came renewed enemy activity in the shape of the doodlebugs. My father, being a fireman, wisely considered that so much magnesium in the house would be gratuitous fuel to any fire caused by the Germans, or otherwise. So, on one of his frequent service visits to the countryside, he quietly dispatched the bomb into a farmer's deep pool.

I still await the headlines in the local paper - "World War Two Bomb Found in Drained Pond!". It may still occur!

Britain's Biggest Explosion

At 11 minutes past 11 on the morning of November 27 1944 - 40 years ago today - the Midlands was shaken by the biggest explosion this country has ever seen.

It was the day Fauld Dump went up; the day that 70 people lost their lives and a day which is seared forever in the memories of those who survived.

In the space of a few seconds, 4,000 tons of bombs blew up, blasting open a crater 400ft deep and 3/4 mile long and completely changing the face of the landscape.

The earth opened and swallowed an entire farm. The farmhouse, out-buildings, wagons, horses, cattle and six people were engulfed leaving a massive rubble filled crater. And in the vast area surrounding it not a tree or blade of grass remained.

Within a radius of 1,400 yards structural damage was caused. Many other buildings and homes with the occupants inside disappeared - some of them never to be seen again.

Of the 70 who died, 19 bodies have never been recovered. Few people in Burton did not hear the explosion or feel the tremor which ran through the earth. As far away as Leicester and Coventry the blast was heard or felt.

Windows were shattered in places miles from the mine yet strangely enough many panes of glass in RAF buildings actually remained intact - such was the freak nature of the blast.

The existence of the great RAF ammunition dump 90ft below the surface where the explosion took place was not officially known to local people.

Wartime security had guarded the secret of the tiers and tiers of bombs which lined the rocky walls.

But it was an open secret and the villagers knew about it with a terrible suddenness when in the peace of mid morning a giant cloud of smoke and debris billowed into the air, the ground heaved and great rocks and stones were flung in all directions.

Great holes were torn in houses, Hanbury Village Hall was ripped apart and the church was severely damaged. In Burton chimney pots were dislodged and the steeples of St John's Church, Horninglow and Christ Church in Moor Street were damaged.

After the explosion the call went out for all the help the surrounding area could give. Fire brigades, service and civilian ambulances, police, civil defence and colliery rescue brigades converged on Fauld.

For several days the search went on among the rubble to release men trapped underground. It was several days however before the full extent of the disaster was known for many men were trapped below ground at the nearby alabaster mine, now British Gypsum.

The original death toll as announced by the then Minister of War was 80, of whom 25 were actually working in the mine at the time. Other estimates range from 70 to 80 - the exact number will probably never be known.

Forty years on the massive crater has been softened by the coverings of nature. Grass and wildflowers grow on what was a barren and torn land.

Time and nature may have combined to heal the scars and soften the memories but the pitted countryside and the history books will forever remind the people of Burton area of: The Day The Dump Went Up.

Burton Mail – *November 27th 1984.*

On that day I was visiting a friend who was over on leave. As we sat chatting there was an ominous subterranean rumble. Our first thoughts were of an accident at one of the pits. The following day, despite wartime censorship, it was widely reported in the local and national press that an ammunition dump had blown up near Burton-on-Trent.

Frank Moore

Peter Wheeldon

On 2nd September 1939 I was returning home to Whitwick after spending the school holidays at Oadby with my aunts. In Leicester, walls of sandbags were being built up around the entrances to the main buildings and there was an unreal feeling of anticipation of the coming war. The train to Coalville stopped for a long time at Bardon and there was the surprising sight of passenger trains queueing for signals on the old line from Nuneaton which had for many years only seen goods traffic. On arriving at Coalville, the platform was packed with children, evacuees brought from Birmingham by the special trains in an apparently well organised operation. Unfortunately, that was as far as it went and volunteers were knocking on doors in the now blacked out streets, still trying to find homes for some of the children until well into the evening.

Over the next few days the unreality of being at war and the expectation of horrific air raids gradually faded. We soon became used to stumbling about in the blackout, school started again and, for most of us, life went on much the same as ever. The opposing armies faced each other in France without much activity and we laughed at the stupidity of Lord Haw Haw on the German radio.

Then, in May, the Germans suddenly invaded Norway, Denmark, Belgium and Holland. The Whitsun holidays had just started and we were highly indignant when the government cancelled the holiday and we had to go back to school. Unbelievably, our army was driven back, the French capitulated and the British were evacuated from Dunkirk.

With the threat of imminent invasion, Churchill called for men between the ages of seventeen and sixty-five to form a defence force to be known as the Local Defence Volunteers and who, in this area, would be expected to oppose any airborne invasion. So, a few days later, being just seventeen, I found myself with a group of about thirty local men gathered in the playground of Whitwick National School, where a few veterans tried to teach us some of the drill they remembered from the 1914-18 war. Two officers had been appointed, a Lieutenant Bruce, manager of Shepshed quarry and Second Lieutenant Sam Perry, the Whitwick tailor. We had no weapons but there was the promise of a few Canadian Ross rifles and one or two people had brought shotguns. We were issued with LDV armbands which were supposed to show that we were recognised combatants and would not be shot if taken prisoner. We then dismissed and repaired to the nearest pub for necessary refreshment, an almost invariable termination of all our activities.

Surprisingly, after a few training evenings, we soon became an efficient unit, thanks to Sam Perry and NCOs Jack Gee, Fred Hall, Wilfred Ward, Frank West and Frank Irons, all old 1914-18 soldiers. Our district covered Whitwick and Thringstone from Gracedieu and Swannington Common to The Oaks and Warren Hills, and we patrolled this area every night from an HQ in a hut in the garden of

The Meadows, Thringstone, then the home of Lt Bruce. This meant an all night duty every three or four days at that time, snatching what sleep we could, with training sessions at least one evening and Sunday morning each week - not a light task for men who still had to turn up for their work the next day. Luckily the summer passed without an invasion, although we had one stand-to in response to a false report that there had been a landing on the East Coast, also the only bombs in the area were one at Snibston and a stick of oil-filled incendiaries which fell across London Road, Coalville, from the railway to Whitwick Colliery, but failed to explode.

As autumn approached, we were issued with denim battledress and greatcoats, so at last we looked a little more like soldiers and we received enough American rifles for all the men, although the ammunition, which was a different size from the British, was in short supply, allowing only five rounds each to be carried by the best shots in the unit. a Lewis machine-gun also materialised and Frank Irons, who had been an armourer in the Royal Flying Corps, was an experienced instructor, teaching us to deal with all the eccentricities of this near obsolete weapon, which had a tendency to jam at vital moments, as we discovered when we tried it out on the Ashby range. We moved into the old station at Whitwick, where now growing supplies of grenades and ammunition could be safely stored and at last we had a stove so we could mash tea and thaw out after a two hour patrol in the freezing nights.

Air raid activity gradually built up and, from the higher ground, we looked over towards Derby and Nottingham in the north and Birmingham and Coventry to the south. With Rolls Royce and the railway works, Derby was defended by large anti-aircraft guns whose shells at times burst high over us, scattering shrapnel. Time and again we heard bombers fly towards Derby, only to veer quickly away to the Birmingham area as the guns opened up. This activity did not worry us unduly, as no bombs fell in the vicinity but one of the Thringstone air raid wardens was greatly concerned that the glow of his pipe might be seen from the air and was very proud of a special metal plate which he had fitted over the bowl. He also lodged a complaint that the glow from our cigarettes would bring down the wrath of the Luftwaffe on Thringstone Green when we occasionally paused there for a smoke, so we were given instructions to use the nearby air raid shelter if we wanted a quick smoke. Our main concern was to detect any parachutists and on two occasions we challenged suspect groups in the middle of the night, one turning out to be some miners gambling with cards off Main Street in Thringstone, and the other the local poachers raiding the Gracedieu Estate.

One night I have never forgotten was in November 1940. We were near the Forest Rock pub from where we had an extensive view towards Birmingham and Coventry, and we were used to seeing the distant flashes of bombs and guns in that direction, but this night the sky around Coventry was ablaze with the light of fires and flares, tracer and gun bursts of all colours. Except for the occasional plane overhead, it was too far away to hear the noise and we had the detached, impersonal state of distant observers. Later, of course, we learned that we had watched the destruction of Coventry. Derby and Nottingham did not suffer as badly as many cities from raids. As well as the guns, Derby had barrage balloons and they had a nightly smoke-screen to conceal them from the air. This was created by large oil-burners set at intervals along the streets which were lit every evening by soldiers as black as chimney sweeps and which gave off masses of thick black smoke. I spent a week in Nottingham on a course and the reek of oil and the black smuts penetrated everywhere, with windows having to be kept closed on the warmest nights, but it did give security from raids.

In the meantime, the force had been re-named the Home Guard and was at last well armed and equipped, although some of the weapons were rather unusual. There were Molotov Cocktails, bottles filled with liquid phosphorous, which ignited on impact and sticky bombs, a type of grenade which stuck to the side of tanks, if you could get close enough. Then we had Sten guns, cheap automatic weapons which fired an uncontrollable hail of bullets and had a nasty habit of going off on their own if they were jolted. The Blacker Bombard was another simple weapon, firing a large mortar bomb. After practising with dummy bombs, we took it to Red Bank at Measham for live tests, where the bomb, instead of exploding on landing, bounced onwards and finished up on the railway line, luckily without exploding.

As the war went on, men in reserved occupations were directed into the Home Guard and some of the younger ones who had joined at the start were called up into the forces. Of these, Aubrey Garratt was killed whilst serving with the Tank Corps and Frank Needham was killed in an air crash in the RAF.

Having completed my engineering course at Loughborough College, I went to the Royal Aircraft Establishment at Farnborough and, except for a short period at the end of the war, did not return for many years, so I did not see my Home Guard comrades again. However, I feel that little tribute has been paid to the volunteers who, in 1940, when invasion was daily expected, were prepared to oppose the enemy with hardly any weapons and, as well as working full-time in the war effort, gave up so much of their own time in the defence of the country. Dad's Army may be amusing but it does not do them justice. Tribute should also be paid to Sam Perry who developed and led the Whitwick Home Guard in the early days and still carried on after his son, John, was killed in action.

Geoff Duckworth

In 1940 I was in the Home Guard, namely the 28th Platoon which was Clutsom and Kemp, where I worked before joining the Navy. One particular manoeuvre that we were on was, I recollect, the capture of Shepshed. All the platoons in the area were, I think, taking part.

My mate had been issued with the first Tommy-gun that we ever had and so we set off from Coalville over the fields crawling through ditches and making believe we were in enemy territory and that sort of thing.

After we'd gone quite a way, a few miles I would think anyway, my mate said he'd lost something off this Tommy-gun which was virtually a criminal offence! So we had to backtrack to find this piece, which we did after about a mile. We carried on with the manoeuvre and as we got into Shepshed we started peering round corners and hiding in entries and generally being furtive. It soon became obvious that there was nobody else from the exercise about, we began to wonder where the hell they had all got to. As we peered round the corner of this house there were two chaps across the road and one of them said, "It's all over mate, where've you been? Your mates are down in the pub playing darts and dominoes." Of course we both felt like fools!

Iris Gleeson nee Storer

The Ace Concert Party

In the early part of the war my father, Fred Storer, and some of his friends formed the Ace Concert Party to help raise money for charity and although some of them had never performed on stage before, devised routines, mostly comedy sketches, and they were joined by younger singers and dancers. My father had been a club singer for quite a few years and before the war was known as The Singing Miner.

There were lots of charities which needed money at this time, from "buying a bed" in Leicester Royal Infirmary to Red Cross Servicemen's Comforts etc and the concert party made a point of entertaining the wounded servicemen either in hospital or by bringing them to Ibstock Working Men's Club, where the ladies would also provide some type of refreshments from their rations.

I joined the party about 1943 when I was eleven years old and there was only one person younger than myself and her name was Ann Burchell. She had been evacuated to our village in 1942 from the London area, along with her family. There were a variety of acts and the best idea would be to give you a description of all the members as they appear on the photograph.

Fred Storer was a singer and sang mostly ballad type songs and sang duets with Mrs Ivy Davies (unfortunately not on the photograph) in the style of the romantic singers of that time, with When I'm Calling You etc. Father also took part in the comedy sketches performed by various members at different times.

Alex Costello organised concerts etc. but was best remembered, I feel, for his part in one of the sketches which was performed about soldiers and how they were interviewed by their sergeant major, and he never used to say a word. He used to wear a long ground sheet type mackintosh, right down to the ground, a tin helmet, with his face covered by white grease-paint. He was then asked how many children he had and would slowly count all his fingers and then bend down and start to count his toes. This used to start great peals of laughter from the audience but he did have a large family. He also joined George Broughton, Arch Bott, my dad and anyone else available in The Operation. A sheet was erected with a light shining from the back of it and in silhouette. There would be several people in white coats, and a patient on the table. There was lots of talking, all ad lib, and all sorts of things would be "extracted" from the "patient", from strings of sausages, to knives, forks, hammers, cleavers and even baby dolls, even though the "patient" was a man. This was so hilarious and I only wish that we could have taken recordings, as it is very hard to convey the merriment of these sketches which could be as long or as short as you wanted them to be, according to the reaction from the audience. My mind goes back with great nostalgia to all these "off the cuff" times.

Archie Bott was a very good comedian, although previous to joining the party he had never done this sort of thing before. He styled himself on the antics of Frank Randle and Norman Evans who were great entertainers of that time. One that I remember most was his "over the garden wall" routine, when he would be dressed in ladies clothes and be leaning over a piano or something which represented the wall, and would be carrying on a one-sided conversation with lots of "ums" etc to show the interruptions by the other person, all ad lib again and so hard to show in words the hilarity of the sketch.

Another favourite of mine was when Uncle Arch came on stage in a motley costume including one white and one black boot, and carrying a violin. Someone would say to him that he had on odd shoes, but he would answer, "No I haven't, I have another pair like this at home." There would be plucking of the strings and eventually he would say that he was going to play "The Sausage Song". When asked what it was, he would reply, "Ah, Sweet Mystery of Life", as during the war we did not always know what was in the sausages. He would then start to play and everyone would be astounded at the sound coming from the violin which he had shown had elastic strings, but as the tune came to an end, my father would walk on stage playing a comb with paper over it, a lovely finish.

George Broughton was the compere and he used to take part in the sketches with the other men and he also used to do a knock-about item with Doreen

Morris. They used to sing "You Made Me Love You" whilst pushing each other around the stage, and making it seem just the opposite to the words.

Chesney Deacon was our pianist and he was very good in his accompaniment and he also used to teach us new songs etc. and help us to get the notes right, as none of us were sight readers, but once the tune was there, it stayed.

Doreen Morris and June Edwards were cousins who used to sing and dance together. This varied from tap to ballet, but June danced the ballet parts. They were very talented and arranged all their own dances etc.

Betty Morris, who I believe was also a cousin to Doreen, also did tap and singing, but she was not a member as long as Doreen and June.

Vera Bott, who was the daughter of Archie, sang ballad type and romantic items, but my favourite was "Ora Pro Nobis" which was a very sad song about a young girl and the death of her mother. Many tears were shed when she sang it with heart rending feelings. Another song was about a young boy who was a crossing sweeper and Vera dressed up as the boy. Vera used to dance with the rest of the girls, including myself, in the company items, such as the opening and ending of the shows. All the girls wore red pleated skirts and white mandarin blouses, all made by my mother or Vera's mother. They were in satin which was one of the fabrics of the day. To offset our costumes, the men were attired in red mandarin shirts and either black or white trousers.

I was a late-comer to the group, along with Ann Burchell, and we both sang similar types of songs, mine in the first place being "I'll Walk Beside You" and "The Rose of Tralee". The favourite one, which Ann was often requested to sing was "My Curly Headed Baby" which she would sing wearing piccaninny clothes and carrying a little black doll.... another tear jerker.

Our ages covered a wide range, as did our talents, but we enjoyed keeping up the spirits of the folks on the home front with our entertainments. We felt we had "done our bit" for the war effort.

We performed in many venues across the county of Leicestershire and also over the borders. In fact, the first place which I journeyed to with the group, was Grendon, and we even went further than that on a couple of occasions - to Dordon, which I am sure is in Warwickshire. These were great adventures as we all used to pile into one large car with all our costumes and props. Taxis at that time were limited to twenty five miles radius, so that to get to Dordon, we had to have other transport for the last few miles, and on cold, foggy and frosty nights it was very scary to drive along lonely country roads with very little light from the car head-lights, as they had to be shielded to stop planes seeing us. You could suddenly come upon a stray cow, horse or sheep or see an owl fly across in front of you like a phantom in the night.

I remember on one occasion going to Bretby Hospital to entertain the wounded soldiers, some of them very serious cases. Those that could be taken in wheel chairs, or could walk, were brought along to one ward and there were also some in their beds. There would be a place at one end for the entertainment to take place. This made us all feel very emotional to see these men who had been so badly wounded whilst ensuring that we were safe in our own homes. To make sure that the rest did not feel left out, we went round the wards talking to the men who could not be moved and several of them gave chocolate to the girls. We did not want to accept, but they insisted. Sweets were rationed during the war and over the years we had varying amounts, from 2 ozs to 4 ozs a week. Not much when you think of how much we eat at one sitting now.

We used to have other things, like liquorice stick, which was like a piece of wood which you could chew and it would last for hours. I am sure that this was not rationed, but I don't remember seeing any for years. I don't suppose it really bothered us much, as everyone was in the same boat.

We were very lucky in this area that we were not constantly bombed, although there were odd bombs that were dropped. These appeared to be when they were on their homeward journey and were getting rid of their load. We could see a glow in the skies when Coventry and Birmingham were being blitzed, and you would hear the sirens and the planes going overhead. They had a different sound to the engines of our planes.

At Christmas time and other events, the members of the concert party would get together to have a party when the food would be supplied by all who attended. My mother would have saved her coupons so that she could obtain a large tin (about 7 pounds) of corned beef. There would be egg custards made from the bantie eggs and other fowls that were kept at the bottom of most gardens, and stored jellies, tinned fruit etc. from all the larders. We did not appear to go without anything, but then I was still a child and my memory would have tinted glasses and only remember the good things. We did not own a piano, but Uncle Arch and Aunt Vera did, so the men would get together and wheel it from their house to ours, in the Avenue on Leicester Road, Ibstock. I used to love it when the piano was at our house, as I could pretend to play.

These events were attended by the members of the party and their friends who were also their supporters, and these would carry on well into the night. The younger members would be put to bed, all in the same house, and we would fall asleep to the sound of songs and merriment below.

A good time was had by all over the years, and we all enjoyed doing something to help ourselves and others to make life a little easier to bear whilst across the world, horrible things were happening, some beyond belief.

These are very fond memories to me and I hope they convey, in some small way, the enjoyment one can receive from trying to help others.

Mrs D H Davis

A Day Out In Coalville In Wartime

We live in Leicester and life during the war of 1939-45, for the average housewife with a young child, was pretty drab. Threats of air raids at any time caused mothers not to leave their children in the care of baby sitters, so they were rarely able to venture out very far.

One day my husband told me he had to go to Coalville on business and was able to use his car. So, if I liked, I and my three year old could go with him "for a treat". I had never been to Coalville before, and envisaged a village with cottages and a few shops - maybe a farm or two, so accepted with gladness.

He dropped us off at the Clock Tower and said he would pick us up there at 4 pm. "BE THERE!" he commanded.

My little lad was enchanted by the bridge over the railway line so we toiled up the steps and took up our places in the middle and stood - and stood. Time passed until we eventually sought the British Restaurant where we had our wartime lunch. I made this spin out as long as possible and then told him we would go and look at the shops. *SHOPS?* What shops? Like everywhere else the windows were either bare or contained cardboard images of what the shops sold. In one was a huge block of purplish coloured, repulsive looking whale meat. So, after a little walk up and down the main street, back we went to our former position on the bridge - and stood there until 4 pm, when we descended to meet my husband and say farewell to Coalville.

I now visit Coalville regularly and have given talks to various organisations over the years. My sister lives within a few miles nowadays and whenever I visit her, we invariably go shopping there. It has grown tremendously and is greatly altered and has many shops and stores. But strangely, that first visit in 1942 still remains vividly in my mind, and in spite of all, we really did enjoy it.

My son, now in his fifty-sixth year, remembers that day perfectly and was so happy to stand on that bridge.

Growing Up

The savagery of war meant nothing to me then
the side I saw in August '39 offered adventure
changed routines
unknown excitement in the weeks ahead.

Disturbing headlines
sparked a homeward dash from Weymouth beach.
Rushed meetings at the school with lists
and cases packed to cover all eventualities.
Two frantic weeks - my father digging
always shelter digging in our small back yard
uncles calling in khaki or handsome Navy blue.

At just turned twelve I knew the world was waiting there for me.
As an evacuee I could escape the umbrella of family restraints.
Escape from urban streets
where playing with rough children was forbidden.
Escape to woods and fields
with wild delights still hidden in the fantasy
promised by weekly tea-time walks
on Children's Hour with Romany.
It was the beginning of my growing up.

By 1945 I understood.
Our home had not survived the bombs though family I loved were still alive.
We celebrated Peace thronged in the City's heart
my part a child no more
but blossoming instead to womanhood.

War hastened childhood days
and teenage traumas were unheard of then
chastened by dreams shattered one by one
my growing-up it seemed was quickly done.

Heather Chandler

Mrs F M Davies

Our Evacuee

What a trauma it must have been for any parent to wave off their children to an unknown "safe" destination during the 1939-45 war, not knowing where they would be staying, or if they would see them again.

My mother was a member of the WVS, helping to billet the load of children from Northfield, Birmingham when they arrived in Ibstock. At the end of day one, no suitable billet could be found for a brother and sister to be placed together. They had a label attached to them saying, "Please do not part them if you can possibly put them together." Mother brought the six year old girl for one night with us and the registrar's wife took the boy. The idea was to have another search for a billet for two on the following day. Still no luck! Mother brought Betty back again and Keith was found accommodation with a family who had a boy the same age - eight years. We had Betty then for five years - we had very little room, but made room. The first night she had with us, she sat on the couch, clutching a very small suitcase, took stock of us all and shed one tear. We never saw another one. We had no mod cons either, one tap across the yard in the wash-house, outside toilet, no bathroom, yet our small house was always warm and comfortable. She loved being with us - called my father Jack, with a twinkle in her eye, and mother Mum. Her own mother was "Mother". Right up to my parents dying, she wrote Dear Mum and Jack.

She made friends at school with two sisters who lived on a farm and played there often with them. After a fortnight, the parents were allowed their first visit and her mum thought it was best perhaps for them to be apart, then they couldn't argue and become a nuisance. Her dad brought her over a "fairy cycle". She travelled miles on that with me. Her brother took the eleven plus examination and, war having almost finished, went home to start his new school. Betty stayed with us a year longer than she need have done whilst she took this exam. She passed too and then went home to grammar school in Birmingham. After leaving school, she trained as a nurse, qualified, then went out to a post in New Zealand. She married out there and produced four children.

Over the years, we have all kept in touch. Many times we visited their Northfield home, also had many lovely holidays in North Wales, visiting and staying in a chalet they had retained, surrounded by eleven acres, including a mountain. Betty's grandparents had lived up there. Her parents kept this chalet and ground after the grandparents' bungalow had to be sold on the occasion of their deaths. Then, when her parents were ready to retire in Birmingham, this same bungalow was up for sale, so they bought it back for their retirement. Many of our friends holidayed up there too, enjoying the beauty and peace right up until June, 1994, when her mother died at ninety three years of age.

After Betty's children grew up, she came over to visit us several times when she visited her parents. Her husband came along once too, and all her children have been over from New Zealand. After her parents, we were always next on the list to be visited whilst she was over. Twice we opened the door to a knock and she stood there. Her in-laws have also been over. Betty and her husband are both retired now.

Her brother Keith and the boy from the family that he was billeted with, still meet each other with their families. After grammar school they chose to do their National Services training, two years before going to university. Herbert lived with them in Northfield whilst doing his degree course in Birmingham University.

All this happiness and pleasure followed this first meeting with our six year old stranger from Northfield.

An Evacuee

Lillian Newell

It was August 1939. I was ten and a half years old. I was attending Mitford Road Junior School, North London with my sister June who was eight. We had two older sisters, Rose aged twelve and Amy aged thirteen, they attended Hornsey Road Secondary School, about a mile from Mitford Road.

The authorities of both schools had informed our parents of the mass evacuation of children which had been planned in the event of war. This was not compulsory, but our parents, having two smaller children, Bertie aged four and Bobbie aged two, thought it safer to let us go.

My three sisters and I were booked for evacuation. We were issued with identity tags to be tied to our coats, and gas masks to be carried at all times. We were told we would be going on a journey sometime.

That time came on Friday 1st September 1939. We had to report to Hornsey Road School at 10.00 am in the morning, it being the point of departure for both schools. This school was very large and I am sure you can imagine the number of children collected there. We were lined up four abreast to walk in columns, escorted by teachers, to St Pancras Railway Station.

At that time and the age we were, we didn't really understand, nor were we prepared for the emotional scenes that confronted us as we left the school buildings and entered the street. It, and surrounding streets were crowded with people crying, some trying to hold us, reluctant to let go. We didn't even see our parents as we left.

At the station we met up with hundreds of children from other schools. The trains were ready and waiting. As we were loaded onto them we could hear the Spitfires overhead, forming a massive circle of protection to escort us to safety. Our parents did not know our destination. We arrived in a small village called Pirton, near Hitchin in Hertfordshire. People were waiting, some just to look, others, who had volunteered to take us into their homes, came to choose who they wanted.

Rose and I were picked together, Amy and June were together.We found we were to live next door to each other and the two families were related. At bed time Rose burst into tears and couldn't be comforted. The family pointed out to her that her younger sister (me) wasn't crying, at which I promptly burst into tears. There was no sleep that night or the following few nights.

On Sunday 3rd September 1939, two days after the evacuation, war was declared. We settled down fairly well in the circumstances. A separate school had been set up for us in the village hall, so we were never actually taught with the village children. They would stand and watch us enter and leave the school, laughing their heads off if one of us fell over, as I did. We never did really mix, there were no lasting friendships made.

My sisters and I used to go for walks together, standing gazing at cows grazing in the fields, watching rabbits chasing each other in and out of the hedgerows. Our particular fascination was watching spiders spinning their webs.

Our dad had his calling-up papers at this time, going into the army. He sent Mum, Bertie and Bobbie with a group of mothers and babies to Luton. Mum hated living in a stranger's house and returned to London after two months.

We were getting unhappy at Pirton. The novelty was wearing off for us and our temporary families. We were being shouted at. Our legs were being slapped for putting our feet on the rails under the dining chairs. The final straw came when we were accused of killing one of the family's chickens. We were scared to touch them! We wrote home and Dad fetched us back to London on his next leave. In London things were quiet. We experienced our first air raid warning in the night. In the dark you can imagine the panic and confusion, some of us being physically sick at the awful wailing noise. It was a false alarm!

A few months later we moved house, still in North London, but at Highbury, quite close to the Arsenal football ground. On the day we moved, the first German bombers broke through our air defences to bomb London. After that the sirens wailed every night, and every night we trekked to the air raid shelter, sometimes from six o'clock in the morning until school time the following day.

One morning the all clear sounded, we came out of the shelter to go to school, suddenly a German plane dived from behind a cloud, very low, and fired its machine guns at us. Mum reacted marvellously, she knocked us flying against a wall, then stood screaming up at the sky. The plane was shot down. The pilot, still very much alive, baled out. We watched his parachute descending as we carried on to school.

There were times when we didn't have time to get to the shelter, then Mum would push us under the sink or the table. Having said all this, we were some of the lucky ones as we didn't get bombed out. We had cooking and washing facilities in the shelter and we practically lived there.

The bombing worsened and there was talk again of evacuation. October 17th 1940 saw us leaving London again, this time all together. The furniture and effects were put in store.

As we rode to the railway station we passed many bombed houses and shops, seeing for the first time the extent of the damage to London. We were diverted several times to avoid large craters in the road.

We arrived in Castle Donington, Leicestershire, late at night. Nobody wanted us, or rather no one wanted seven of us. Mum wouldn't let us be separated. We were then taken on to Hemington about a mile away. There we waited, outside the school, while people looked us over. One lady, Mrs Dakin, had a small son Christopher, she wanted to take Bertie and Bobbie as companions for him, but Mum wouldn't let them go.

It was getting quite late, so it was decided to bed us down in the school. As we picked up our luggage a lady named Mrs Wardle came and said she would take us all. She was housekeeper to a local farmer, Charlie Clifton who lived, unmarried, in a very large farmhouse called Grange Farm, Hemington.

We lived at Grange Farm for quite a few months, by then really getting hooked on country life. This was due to the total acceptance of us by Charlie and Mrs Wardle and her family who lived and worked at the Grange. They all had a great sense of humour. The first morning after our arrival we discovered where milk came from in an unexpected way. We were sent to fetch milk from the dairy. Finding no one there we ventured into the cow shed and were met by streams of wet, warm liquid in our faces. Charlie and his men were hand milking, pulling the cows teats and aiming at us. This was only one of many tricks played on us. We were accepted by the village as a whole and by falling into the village brook we were automatically christened Hemington-ites.

Later Charlie rented Mum one of his farm cottages next to the farm. Dad came to us on his leaves from the army and in September 1942 our youngest brother

Doug was born at Lockington Hall. The hall had been turned into a Maternity Home for London mums to have their babies in peace, away from the bombs. To this day Doug remains unimpressed by his aristocratic birthplace.

When the war ended, we had the opportunity to return to London, but we stayed in Hemington. Amy, Rose and later myself went back to London to work. Amy married and stayed there. Rose and I came back to Hemington, although I now live at Castle Donington.

Denis Baker

Get Into The Pantry Away From the Bombs.

I was nine when war broke out and the first thing I remember doing is going to the Baths Hall, I think, to get my gas mask and its cardboard case. There were long queues of children and we all had fun talking to each other in our masks and blowing so as to make rude noises as the air escaped around the side. Later Dad had a service type which had a long valve thing in the centre, between and just below the eyes, which could make even better sounds. I recall thinking at the time what a fiddle it all was that the Government must have planned a war a long time before in order to have time to make all those masks. Had they only gone to war now that they had enough of them? It never really dawned on me that the masks were intended possibly to save our lives until I started to collect fag (cigarette) cards about 'Air Raid Precautions'.

Inspired by these cards (and no doubt by newspapers) we went about preparing our 'Front Line' defences by sticking black insulating tape over the inside of our windows, producing a mock leaded-light effect. Some enterprising firm produced thin transparent sheeting printed with stained-glass window effects and Mum was always one of those who liked to set a trend so the next Saturday we visited 'Woolies' to get some for our parlour window. I spent a long time getting the insulating tape off and Mum fitted the new material in place but never really managed to get the creases out. At last we were ready to meet the Hun.

Our street games immediately took on a war urgency. On the Scotlands brickyard we dug trenches, using old corrugated iron sheets to make bunkers and command posts as seen at the Pictures. Our weapons were automatic rapid-fire rifles and Bren guns fashioned from high quality broom stales and bits of wood scrounged from Grudging's wood yard nearby. Our rate of fire was dependent on our ability to say "da-da-da" rapidly and by the amount of breath we had to sustain it. We would occasionally have pitched battles with enemy hordes, in the shape of the Oxford Street gang. Both sides would equip themselves with live ammunition (brick-ends) and on the agreed signal both sides would make war from their trenches across a no-mans-land carefully measured at a distance slightly more than the flight of a grenade (brick-end) thrown by the average nine or ten year old. Some over-average throwers could just reach the opposing lines

41

and some of us received war wounds (in the form of bruised legs) resulting from ricochets (bounces off the ground). The battle ended when all ammo had been used and we all then shared our ginger pop before collecting ammo for the next battle.

At home much time was spent in gathering together (hoarding) as much non-perishable food as possible and we kids were dispatched at speed to stand in queues whenever news of the latest source of supply reached the neighbourhood. Tinned fruit, tinned salmon, jars of meat paste, rice, pearl barley, sugar of anything similar was carefully hidden away in wardrobe drawers, attics, cellars etc. and much of it was so carefully preserved that it came into use for the VE day street parties.

Blackout covers for all windows were rapidly mackled together from roof laths and roofing felt and fixed every evening on the outside of the windows. This was OK in the winter but in the summer it made the house unbearably hot and so Mum got hold of some thick black fabric to make interior curtains which rapidly replaced the outer covers.

Then the evacuees arrived. One evening a large group of weepy children cam along the road and were allocated one-by-one to houses. Mum went out to collect our boy but the man explained that he'd had these twins, who he did not want to separate, and so my aunt next door had the boy twin and Mum had the girl. What a shock to my system! I had not, to that time, had anything to do with girls except for two tomboys who were neighbours and who I never considered as girls. Now I had a foster sister, who seemed to be always crying for home, to put up with. The routine of the house was changed but fortunately Ruth and her brother, Roy Skelcher, settled into our lives and stayed with us for a number of years. Later, at the height of the blitz, we were asked if we could provide respite care for their mother's aged friend, who was partially paralysed and thus unable to be taken to shelter from the bombs. Mum immediately agreed and Mrs. Agnes Rogers of Hall Green became an honorary aunt in residence for a long period. She was a dear old lady who, although badly bomb shocked, was ready to play and have a joke with us children.

Bombing raids raised much interest since Coalville seemed to have been on the Luftwaffe's 'super highway'. My Dad was a street warden and had to be outside when there was an alert. I remember how he organised us in the pantry under the stairs with instructions to "Get into the pantry to stay away from the bombs" until he told us to come out. How Mum, Ruth and myself, and later Mrs. Rogers, were able to fit in such a small place I now cannot imagine but for quite a number weeks we did so when night alerts sounded. However, as no bombs fell, everyone soon became rather indifferent to the danger and we stayed in the passage outside the pantry instead. After a while Dad used to let me go out onto Forest Road bridge on moonlit nights to see the bombers come over.

First you could hear the threatening, immediately recognisable, vrm-vrm-vrm noise of many engines and see at a distance searchlights crossing to and fro and flashes of ack-ack in the sky. Then in the moonlight you could see thousands (well perhaps a hundred) aircraft flying straight in line to Bardon Hill where they separated to bomb either Derby, Coventry, Birmingham or Nottingham. A short time afterwards you could see the sky light up over those unfortunate cities. When Derby was attacked you could hear tremendous explosions as the planes arrived which Dad explained were due to Big Bertha naval guns being used to attack planes. Whether this was accurate I never found out but some mornings, although we hadn't had a raid, it was possible to pick up shrapnel in the streets of Coalville which was said to come from shells fired by those guns.

One day during a lull in the Blitz my Dad took us by car into Birmingham to see if my Aunt, who lived in Small Heath, was all right. There were dozens of barrage balloons everywhere in parks and cemeteries and the damage was incredible. There had been a small raid the night before and the streets were a mass of hoses with small fires here and there and water gushing from mains in fountains. I saw a school so badly damaged that only one wall was left standing and a map of the world still hanging precariously from the picture rail. A small amount of floor remaining in place supported a couple of desks which looked about to fall at any time. Fortunately Aunt's house was undamaged apart from broken windows, despite a land-mine dropping in a nearby street. It damaged about sixty houses by blowing out all windows, doors and interior partition walls and removing the roofs. Many people were killed by the blast.

Fortunately Aunt Maude was quite 'perky' and gave us a cup of strong tea when water was temporarily restored. We also visited Mrs. Skelcher who was also safe and well and we left Birmingham, rather foolishly I thought, as it started to get dark. The car's headlights, never very good in those days, were made worse by the blackout mask which allowed only a narrow flat ruler of light to shine horizontally in front. We made slow progress so that we were only just clear of the city when the alert sounded. As we drove away we could see and hear at close hand the bombs exploding and ack-ack guns firing. I will always remember that first close brush with the real enemy.

Some time afterwards the 'Blitz of Coalville' began. One night we were laid in the passage as usual, having been raised by the siren, when Dad came rushing in through the back door shouting "Everybody flat on the floor". We were all so startled that we obeyed and simultaneously heard the whistle of bombs falling. The next thing I remembered was being thrown along the hall and into a heap with the rest of the family. A stick of bombs had fallen in a line, starting in the Convent field and finishing in Coalville Park, and since our house was opposite

Convent Drive we caught the blast. Our anti-blast stained-glass windows and insulating tape held and we could never understand why! Dad later said that he had seen a train coming through Coalville East junction puffing out sparks just as German planes were returning. He had heard a plane start to dive and ran in to warn us and our neighbours.

There was great excitement next morning as we went to examine the damage. There were two craters and slightly damaged hedges in the Convent field, one crater in rail track outside London Road Cemetery, the wall blown out of the dentist Brown's house on London Road and one wall destroyed in Coalville Park. A bomb, larger than the others, fell at the far side of the Park, a short distance away from the Colliery powder magazine and did not explode thank goodness. Some boys later found the bomb while playing, possibly fighting another battle using the crater as the trenches, and it was removed. The 'second phase' of the blitz occurred some time later when a much larger bomb fell one night in Mr. New's farmyard on Owen Street and fortunately didn't explode. Several people heard it fall but it couldn't be found until sometime later when it was dug out from a great depth, defused and put on show in the foyer of the Rex Cinema. You were invited buy a 6d (2½p) saving stamp to stick on it and it was then going to be dropped back on Germany.

In the home things were on ration but the only thing which really concerned most children was the shortage of sweets. I remember standing on Saturday morning in the queue outside Jobling's in Belvoir Road to collect my ration. I always went there because the lady in the shop knew my Mum and always gave me a few more sweets than the ration. These I allocated to myself over the following week but never seemed to manage until the following Saturday. To make butter go twice as far I remember Mum mixing it with cornflour and milk which produced a thin spread for bread and which could not be detected by kids under the apple and blackberry or marrow jam we made in large quantity, sugar permitting.

There always seemed some special fund raising to do. Warship Week, Spitfire Fund, Salute the Soldier Week and others seemed to be in the news and we kids got involved in whatever way we could. My cousin Derek, evacuee Roy and myself built a stage out of old orange boxes, erected scenery out of old curtains and prepared a concert to present to the locality and successfully raised 6/6d (32½p) for the Red Cross fund. Our efforts were recorded in the Coalville Times and we were given more by people who were not able to attend. Our next effort, this time assisted by my cousin Alan, was for Mrs. Churchill's Aid to Russia Fund. Much to our parents' subsequent dismay we stripped our gardens of flowers and sold them in bunches in the street to passers-by. We were rewarded with a personal letter from Mrs. Churchill and again a mention in the Coalville Times.

In 1941 I went to Ashby Grammar School and the war became a little more alive for me as one of the teachers would comment on significant events, often bemoaning the fact that we could not go on summer camping holidays to the continent. Thus we followed with mixed interest the North Africa campaign and the landings in Italy and I remember him rushing into our classroom to tell us about D-Day.

I believe I knew of this day before it happened for several of us had been hitching lifts for several months in American Army lorries and being given presents of undreamed-of goodies to take home. The tinned fruit cakes became on of our regular luxuries, I always had loads of sweets and Dad plenty of 'Camel' fags. I didn't like gum so I used to swap that for other candies with a pal who was addicted to the stuff.

From conversations with the GIs it became apparent that the invasion was near and they were guessing the date and place for several months. The convoys suddenly ceased and a few nights later I was awakened by the sound of many planes heading south, which I suppose was part of the Airborne Fleet. So the D-Day announcement came as no surprise but I missed the goodies.

In my early years at Ashby Grammar School I joined the Hugglescote Scouts and had my first holiday away from my family in distant fields (actually Gopsall Hall). There I was introduced to the wonders of camp-fire cooking and became a dab-hand at producing rather grey Dampers which tasted superb spread with treacle or jam. One morning as we lay awake in our bell-tents, just aroused by the bugle call, we heard a terrific whining noise and being ordered into the adjacent woods by a screaming Patrol Leader we emerged to see the underbelly of a German fighter plane diving down and to hear the chatter of its machine guns as it attacked the Army at the nearby Hall. As far as I know no-one was hurt but it left a lasting memory for me especially as we began to realise we might have been the target.

One of the teachers, Mr. Ramsell I believe, was the one to tell us of Germany's capitulation and we had a holiday. As the street parties were arranged it was announced that fireworks, prepared for sale before the war, would be on sale and I remember visiting a small shop on Forest Road, Champion's I think, who had the most amazing collection I have ever seen for sale.

Films about the war became essential viewing. News of and, particularly, the sight of the horrors of concentration camps and later of the Japanese atrocities really disturbed me. I had seen war as somewhat heroic, even during the Blitz, but for the first time I began to understand why Dad never wanted to talk about the First World War. As news came through about the atom bombs my thoughts were "Serve them right".

R G Woolman

The War Years 1939-1945

"The day war broke out" to quote Rob Wilton, I was twelve years old. I had just completed my first year at Coalville Grammar School. The youngest boy of four children, my older brother fourteen years older and my younger sister, eleven years older. All three were married and had left home. We lived in a small terraced cottage in one of two rows in Ashburton Road, Hugglescote. These had at one time been owned by Bardon Quarry who let them to their employees. My father was employed by the quarry when he married in about 1910.

He later worked at Ibstock Colliery until he was badly injured there in an accident in 1926/27. After many months in hospital he recovered, but not sufficiently to follow his normal employment. The Leicestershire and Derbyshire Mine Owners Association paid him a modest sum of weekly compensation which was his sole source of official income until 1940. He obtained a wartime job as a firewatcher on night shift in a leather factory in Leicester. My mother was very close to her younger spinster sister Molly, who was employed in what in those days was called "good service" in London. She was cook to a well known stage and screen actress whose husband was a director of The Bank of England. This position gave her the opportunity to be generous to her younger relations. In late August 1939, Aunt Molly took me on holiday to Ramsgate. Only my second such sojourn to the seaside. We joined friends of hers, Bill and Amy Butler, with their son Billy who was about the same age as me. With the war on the horizon it wasn't the best time to have a holiday. Traders were panicking and selling all they had for next to nothing. Council employees were filling sandbags on the beach. Kids were having the time of their lives, helping with their buckets and spades.

On Saturday 2 September, we left for London and stayed overnight at the Butlers' flat. On the Sunday morning we listened to Mr Chamberlain's address to the nation with its declaration of war. Billy's school were already evacuated. Since he had missed this, it was decided that he would come home with us until it could be arranged for him to join his school.

We were sitting in the train on St Pancras Station when the sirens went for the first time. As we didn't know what to do, we sat and waited. People were running about and the barrage balloons started to go up. Eventually things calmed down, the all clear went and the train pulled out of the station. All because one unidentified plane had approached the south east coast.

Very little changed in the first six months of the war. School went on as normal. One minor change was in school uniform. Instead of having a new cap each term at a cost of three shillings and sixpence, we were allowed to make them last as long as possible, even being allowed to have them cleaned. This was a big saving as my grant for the whole five years was only two pounds. Sports and PT kit was made to last much longer. There were, however, some staff changes at school. Mr Hill, sports and PT master, was called up. Mr Smith, maths master, who was on the Reserve of Officers, was recalled. Miss Wilks, who also took PT and maths,left to join the Education Department, in an administrative capacity. Miss Salt eventually left to go into research in industry. New staff were Miss Smith, PT, Miss Wells, maths and Miss Bunguard, commerce.

All men of military age were required to register for military service and depending on occupation, were called up. A form of conscription had started just before the war. Young men were called to a militia for six months. This was quickly changed to the duration of hostilities which in many servicemen's minds was very elastic.

One of my early school friends was a farmer's son. The farm was in Dennis Street and in common with many, is no more. We usually did our homework together on the big kitchen table before exploring or helping on the farm. Whilst we had great fun we also did regular jobs. We cleaned cow sheds, washed down yards, cleaned milk floats and cut up turnips for cattle food. One regular job was delivering milk to retail customers. The milk was delivered by pony and trap and measured from cans and churns direct into the customers' jugs. Only the big boys delivered in bottles.

We also helped at haymaking and harvest time. One job I remember, where I was taught a never forgotten lesson about horses. The farmer was drilling a field of turnips. It was dry and the soil was sandy. The drill sat on top of the furrow on two iron wheels which looked like large cotton reels. The farmer guided the drill whilst one of us lead the horse and the other sat on the drill. When we reached the end of the furrow the whole thing was turned round. I was leading the horse and reached this point. I pulled the horse round when it instantly put its great iron shod hoof on my foot. Fortunately the ground was soft and I survived with only minor damage. I pushed in future!

One of the major changes in the locality in the early part of the war was the influx of evacuees. These were from all levels and they were billeted on local families. My elder sister had two in addition to her own two children, in a two up and two down cottage in Donington le Heath. We also had a complete girls' grammar school from the Birmingham area. This school, as far as I can remember, was sharing Coalville Grammar School. The evacuees included all sorts. One clear memory is of standing against the top handgate to the recreation field in Ashburton Road and watching a small red haired evacuee, scruffily dressed, looking a bit like Just William. He had a catapult which would have made every boy in the neighbourhood green with envy. He then smashed every insulator on the telegraph pole (at least twenty). He then moved on to the next.

Other tales abounded. One classic was of the small boy being prepared for bed, who was supposedly sewn into his vest with a label not to remove until May.

The phoney war went on. A lot of the evacuees persuaded their parents to fetch them home despite the obvious dangers. As the war progressed, we began to realise that things were not the same. Air raid wardens were soon apparent with their constant vigil for breaches of the blackout regulations. The church bells stopped ringing. Every day things disappeared eg bananas, oranges, lemons and other tropical fruit.

As there were no freezers, most foods were seasonal. Chickens did not lay in the winter. Housewives were encouraged to pickle eggs, salt beans and preserve fruit, either by making jam or bottling. Dig for Victory was part of the Ministry of Food's regular battle cry. Where possible people kept a pig and neighbours helped by saving scraps for feeding. Of course the meat and offal was shared. Rabbits were another source of meat and the grammar school at one time kept rabbits in the cricket pavilion.

The ARP issued gas masks and there were three types. The standard type was issued to adults and the larger children. The Mickey Mouse type was issued to toddlers. The one for babies and smaller children was all enveloping with the child sitting inside and having a hand operated pump. The standard model was issued in a sturdy cardboard box on string for carrying on the shoulder. This was not good enough for most of us and of course soon special carrying cases were available, made of plastic or even leather. They offered very little protection especially as they were kicked as we walked along. We were constantly in trouble with the head warden who had to make the repairs.

Newspapers were small to conserve imported newsprint. Our other sources of news were the wireless and the newsreels,changed to weekly at the cinemas. The wireless was the most current, but I suppose we were only told what it was thought we ought to know. The cinema was our main source of entertainment. The wireless was close behind. Programmes I remember were Band Wagon with Arthur Askey and Dickie Murdoch, Garrison Theatre with Jack Warner, Music Hall, Monday Night at Eight and Saturday Night Theatre. We were exhorted to eat more vegetables by Lord Woolton and have a healthy diet by the Radio Doctor. We also used to listen to Germany Calling with Lord Haw Haw.

By 1940 things had deteriorated. Air raids hotted up with the blitz on London and other cities. We were pushed out of Europe and left very much alone. We evacuated the BEF from Dunkerque and were very much at bay. Our personal involvement was very little as this was going on all round us at Derby, Birmingham and Coventry.

Some families were personally touched and I recall several locals who lost a son, either killed or a prisoner of war. Our age group was hardly touched. We went to school, did our homework and generally carried on as normal. Our evening activities were curtailed by the blackout so opportunities for getting up to mischief were very few.

Where it came from I don't know, but a group of us, both sexes, were encouraged to join the Youth Service Corps. It was partly social and partly voluntary effort. One of our main functions was to collect waste paper for recycling. When I think of some of the material which was given to us I could weep. We collected, in addition to newspapers and magazines, hard back books, some of which were probably collectors' items. Encyclopaedias, some were probably a hundred years old. We stored the paper in Wells Stone Masons Yard in Central Road. We were also responsible for keeping clean a brand new mobile canteen for use by the WVS in case of an emergency. We were supervised by Miss Wells, by now one of the teachers.

One of the consequences of the war situation was the start of the Local Defence Volunteers. Initially they were recognised by an arm band with LDV on it. They were drilled with an old shotgun, air rifle or broom handle. Eventually they were formalised with commissioned and non-commissioned officers, uniforms and arms. Platoons were formed all over the district with companies such as Pegsons and the mines, as well as villages. Hugglescote had its own which was headquartered at the old scout drill hall in Dennis Street. Officers were Captain Veasey and Lieutenant Luther. Both were World War One veterans. I knew Roland Luther best through his children, some of whom were of my age group. Indeed one of his sons was at the grammar school with me. Roland was a miner and political activist for many years, serving on the County Council. He was very proud of his war service and paraded into his eighties with highly polished medals at the annual Armistice Service.

The NCOs I remember were Sergeant Ray Edwards, who was married to my younger sister and Corporal Parker who live in Belvoir Road. They were both miners and Ray was a former member of the Territorial Army. I spent many hours watching the parades and we took special interest when they were practising and dismantling the Lewis Machine Gun.

Sunday morning was given over to manoeuvers on completion of which they usually retired to the Castle Inn to exercise their elbows. My father had been unemployed since 1927 and he supplemented his small compensation income by acting as one of Hugglescote's four highly illegal bookmakers runners. They worked for the Coalville office of a Loughborough bookmaker. In those days only credit and on course betting was legal. Cash betting off the course was against the law. The runner collected the bets either in the local pub or at home. Bets of threepence and sixpence each way were not unusual. Each runner had a "clock". This was a leather bag with a timing device which stopped when the bag was closed. The bets were put in the bag before the first race. Prior to the war, Joe, the Coalville manager, drove round the area collecting the clocks but as the war progressed, petrol became rationed. As a result the clocks had to be taken to the Coalville office. Wartime racing became restricted to Saturdays and it fell to me to take the four clocks from Hugglescote. For this, Joe's secretary gave me two shillings. Due to the illegality of this operation and my tender age, I carried the clocks under my library books in a small leather bag. During this period, one of my regular school friends was a police sergeant's son.

All sorts of things were being done to supplement rations. One way was to grow soft fruit. Where the Gate Inn car park is now were allotments where we rented a good sized piece for five shillings a year. Before we could start, I being the youngest, had to pick off about half a ton of stones. However, it did produce good crops, the best of which was about forty pounds of strawberries a year. We were allowed sugar above the ration to turn these into jam.

Local farmers in those days were sociable, not being as affluent as they are today. One such farmer in Donington had a fifteen acre field, used before the war for air displays. This was ploughed and fertilised before being planted with potatoes. The farmer sold the potatoes by the row, the buyer being responsible for the eventual recovery and removal. We had wireworm infested spuds running out of our ears for a very long time. There were no well ventilated barns and paper sacks to enable potatoes to be stored for months. In those days potatoes were stored under straw covered by earth in what were called clamps. We were allowed by the farmers, after the wheat crop had been harvested, to gather the fully headed stalks which had missed the reaper. This was known as gleaning and the sharp straw played havoc with your hands, particularly the finger ends, making them bleed.

The sacks of wheat were hand thrashed and the resulting corn used for feeding the chickens. Sometimes, however, mum would make frumerty (or thrumerty), a sort of milk pudding using wheat instead of rice.

We had two air raids in the area that I recall. There was the much publicised unexploded bomb which was discovered in New's coal yard in Owen Street. This was very much a nine day's wonder as it was of considerable size. The other was dropped one night in the field at the end of the cottages in Tweentown, Donington. It made a large crater and broke most of the windows for a long way round. One chicken coop complete with chickens disappeared entirely.

Most people in work, and there was fairly full employment, appeared to be involved in war work of some kind. The local engineering firms were making war supplies. There was a factory in Owen Street making aircraft parts. The engineering equipment at the Technical College was similarly occupied. Of course most of the machinery in the older factories was steam driven so the mines were working three shifts to supply them, the gas making plants and steel works. The UK mining industry was producing two hundred million tons of coal a year and employed over half a million men.

My elder sister's husband, Walter, was a miner on permanent night shift. She had two children and I spent many nights with them. My nephew and I shared a bed with, against the rules, the dog on the bed and the kitten in it. We had sporadic air raid warnings and spent the night under the stairs or the table. The warnings were usually for aircraft on the way to Derby, Birmingham or Coventry. The raids we did have were when bombers dropped undelivered bombs on the way home. The next morning when Walter came off shift, we raided his snap bag for Waggon Wheels or other goodies from the pit canteen.

As I lived in Hugglescote and Charlotte lived in Donington, after I had done my homework I walked the half mile or so between us. It was my normal practice to walk across the fields even under blackout conditions. It was usually easy but on this particular night we had a thick fog. This was common in the winter as so much coal was burned. Very bravely I set off and shortly I was lost completely. After stumbling around, bumping into cows, I almost fell into the brook. I followed the brook to the Corner Pin, ending up in Manor Road, which I then followed to my sister's house.

As the war went on, my age group lead very much a normal life, except for rationing of food, sweets etc. Our evening activities were curtailed by the blackout. Rationing had been there before the war by sheer absence of money due to the recession. Work had been very short. The cinemas were still open and with the eventual arrival of Sunday opening, were changing programmes three times a week, giving us the possibility of six shows a week, money permitting.

Hugglescote had a nine hole golf course south of Grange Road. It was laid out following the brook towards the Leicester railway line (Bardon). There was a club house just off Grange Road. As it was laid out over farm land following the brook, the farmer's sheep cropped what would now be fairways. The greens were fenced to keep off the sheep. A source of income was looking for lost balls, very often before they were lost! Eventually the South Colliery spoil bank began to encroach on the course. The farmers were pressed to plough more land and produce more food, so eventually the golf course was no more. The club house was abandoned and fell into disrepair. It was later pulled down. A sad end when you think of the demand for such facilities today.

One outcome of the times was the military orientated Youth Organisations. The ATC, Army Cadets and the Girls Training Corps were formed. We had them all in the Coalville area. The 1188 Squadron of the ATC was one of the earliest in the country and still exists. The grammar school had its own squad, lead by Mr Broomhall as Pilot Officer, Flight Sergeant Parker and Corporal Ellis whose father was a dairyman in Belvoir Road. All the organisations supplied uniforms so most of us at school joined the ATC. We had drill parades and met in the physics lab to learn the rudiments of navigation. We had a derelict Hawker bi-plane fighter in the playing field to explore. The engine was eventually removed and installed elsewhere where we learned a little about engineering.

One of the perks of being an air cadet was that we had the opportunity of a week on an operational airfield at the cost of about 7s 6d. We were lucky enough to go to Swinderby in Lincolnshire, a station operating Lancaster and Manchester Bombers on the thousand bomber raids on Germany. Our time was spent on seeing how a wartime airfield worked. We were shown all aspects of the operation and had a great time. Some were lucky enough to go up on test and training flights. This was not my lot. I did however help to load bombs for operational raids. The bombs were collected from the bomb dump, fused, and loaded on special carriers or, when these ran out, flat farm trailers. Then they were towed by tractor with us riding on them, to the bombers, where we helped to hoist them into the bomb bay.

The other thing we did, and I never did in my later service days, was to volunteer for fatigues in the sergeants' mess cook house. Most of them were aircrew and as such were treated quite correctly as Lords of Creation. They fed accordingly and so did we. Our stay was crowned by an ENSA show in the Garrison Theatre. This was a play by Anthony Kimmins called "While Parents Sleep", for its time quite risque, especially for fifteen year olds.

In the same period the school organised a harvest camp. About thirty pupils, all male, with five teachers, loaded onto a lorry and drove to Staunton Harold where we set up camp. We were situated in a field near Lount Wood adjacent to an abandoned brick yard. The Ferrers Arms was across the road. The land was owned by Frank Hodges, landowner, mine owner and I believe Member of Parliament. I must say, the staff were very efficient and after erecting the tents, set up a superb field kitchen from brick, scrap metal and brickyard clay. They also set up ablutions including latrines and we soon had a well run establishment.

Miss White, Miss Salt and Mr Williams produced some great food during the month the camp was operating. Our prime function was to provide cheap labour to the farmers of the district. Pay was sixpence an hour up to fourteen years and eightpence an hour after that. We were given a packed lunch each day and allocated jobs.

My first was pulling a field of horse beans for cattle food. The normal method of harvesting was with a reaper as with wheat. This particular crop had podded very low on the stems and such a method would have been wasteful. The field was on a gradient and we joined a group of pensioners from the village. We went up one row and down the next. The oldies followed us making sheaves and stooking them to dry. They only worked uphill as they didn't have to bend so far. The wisdom of age? The crop was full of thistles which scratched your bare arms and tore the knees out of your trousers. The jobs varied. I remember pulling flax for making linen and linseed oil at Coleorton. I also worked on the Countess Ferrers' market garden on what is now the Staunton Harold Garden Centre. The hall was occupied by the military and the Ferrers family lived in the vicarage. The current Earl Ferrers who was, like us, a schoolboy is now a government minister in the House of Lords.

The hardest job I had was working in a large wheatfield. After stooking the sheaves and completely drying them, they were collected on trailers and carts. They were then delivered to the stack and fed to the mechanical elevator which lifted the sheaves to the top. I, all five stone of me, was catching the sheaves and tossing them to the burly farmer who was building the stack. The heads were laid inwards to protect them from the rain whilst awaiting thrashing. I was soon in trouble for throwing them the wrong way. All this for sixpence an hour and a cheese and tomato sandwich.

On completion of our day's work we walked or cycled back to camp. After washing (in cold water from a cattle trough) we had our main meal of the day. These were quite substantial and well cooked. After eating we washed up and had a games session before entertaining the curious villagers with songs around the camp fire. And so to bed.

I would imagine our parents were considerably out of pocket after a month, due to wear and tear on our clothes. We walked home at weekends, where we came in contact with hot water for the first time for weeks. We had to walk because the only bus went from Ashby, an equal walk away. We paid for our keep and all we had to show for a month's work was one pound. We returned home very tired after a month. When holidays finished we returned to school and normal activities. The older male pupils were offered the chance to act as firewatchers on school premises. This entailed staying overnight in the domestic science room and patrolling, looking for possible incendiaries during warnings. We were supervised by a member of staff and did a week at a time for three shillings a session. Very welcome cash in a constant famine.

The harvest camp would have been in the summer of 1942 as I don't recall another. A group of us did, however, go to a local farm to weed a field of turnip seedlings, so the farmer could thin them out. Wages were the same as we had at the camp. We made the job last until the farmer rumbled us and supervised the job until done. A pity as we were doing quite nicely, both from the cash point of view and missing school. At the end of the summer term 1943 my school days ended.

There were no careers masters in those days, and unless you were going into the sixth form or university, you were left to your own devices as far as employment was concerned. I had an ambition to work on a newspaper. My brother was cartoonist on the forces newspaper, The Billet, published by Jack Hussey, who was Coalville representative for the Leicester Mercury. He tried for some weeks to obtain for me a junior post with the Mercury, without success.

Following some family pressure I had to abandon this ambition. I therefore went to the Juvenile Employment Exchange in Leicester and was sent to a firm of worsted spinners in Sarah Street, Leicester and started there as office junior the following Monday in the counting house. The company occupied, and still does, the oldest business premises in Leicester, having been established since the early part of the eighteenth century. The office I worked in was real Dickensian, with high desks and stools. The male staff of military age had gone with few exceptions. The remaining men were in their early or late forties. My own two companions were over seventy and both preferred to stand at the high desks rather than use the stools.

It was a friendly company, both managers and staff, although in common with most companies employing clerical labour, the pay was never generous and this continued for many years to come. I was paid twenty five shillings a week plus six shillings and sixpence bus fare for five and a half days a week, 9am to 5.30pm and 9am to 12 noon on Saturdays. My day started at 7.30am when I either walked to Coalville or caught my first bus. From Coalville I caught the 7.55am to Leicester, arriving at about 8.30am at St Margaret's Bus Station. I then walked a mile to Campbell Street sorting office to collect the mail bag. I then walked just over a mile to the office arriving about 9am. The Company Secretary and I then opened the mail, listing cash receipts ready for the arrival of the Managing Director. He then decided who had what and I distributed it to the responsible people.

My other duties varied, but included mailing, wages, banking, some ledger and statement work, and keeping the boardroom stocked with soda water and other mixers. I also bought stationery, having my own order book. I used this also when scouting the town for board room supplies, both of the smoking and liquid kinds.

In the office I quickly learned how to use the calculating machines which were not electronic and extremely hard work. Over the next two years I learned more about the office routines and by the time I was approaching my military service, I was earning the magnificent sum of two pounds and five shillings a week and paying two shillings in Income Tax. With hindsight I realize that although I had been pointed to my job by the employment people, there had been no pressure to join a company engaged in war work. I suppose we did make essential supplies, being woollen and worsted yarns which were made up into clothing. In no way did it compare with heavy engineering. Some of my contemporaries obtained employment locally eg Pegsons, Burgess's, Clutsom and Kemp, Wolsey or in the mining or brick making industry. A large proportion however, like me, commuted daily to Leicester by bus. I would guess there were about sixty in my year.

Out of those who did not stay on to the sixth form or go into further colleges or university, five were on the same bus as myself. Out of these, three worked in the County Library HQ and one in the County Architect's department. I was the only one in industry. Tell me what has changed in fifty years.

One added attraction in the locality was the fair, which was on the fairground in Owen Street where it became a permanent fixture for most of the war years. The coconut shies became a second source of unrationed chocolates and we had a friend who was very proficient at winning at sixpence a go. We then had chocolates for our Saturday night at the cinema where we went after lining up into Owen Street or Margaret Street depending on which cinema we patronised. The third cinema, the Grand, was closed at the beginning of the war and was used for a store I believe for bearings. The other two cinemas, The Rex and The Regal, by now opened on Sundays as well.

Over the next two years very little changed for the young who had little involvement directly, unless through the family or war work. I know I didn't read the newspapers a lot. I did listen to the wireless and heard news and Winnie's speeches. When I had the money I went to the cinema as often as I could and couldn't avoid the newsreels.

We played football and cricket and stayed out at night as long as we could see. Most of us by this time had bought second-hand bikes and used them at weekends to see some of the countryside. Shortly after starting work, my father who was then working on Desford Aerodome for Reid and Seigrist, died from pneumonia. He was so weak from his previous injuries that the then available treatment was no good. There were no antibiotics as we know them today. He was only sixty-three. My mother, who was crippled in one arm from an earlier fall, could not go to work. The pension in those days was ten shillings a week. She did, however, carry on the betting business, helped by Walter who collected the bets in the local. Additionally my Aunt Molly gave up her service job and came to live with us. She worked as a cook in a shoe factory in Shepshed. We weren't rich but we got by.

My mother was an excellent manager after years of practice and I don't remember ever being without some money when the need arose in the family. We were never hungry. We were getting a little older and possibly a little more responsible. 1944 arrived and the war news when we noticed, was getting better. Additionally we were slowly approaching the day we had to register the first step towards National Service.

Soon D Day arrived with the Invasion of the Continent. The Blitz changed somewhat from bombers to V1 and later V2 rockets, and as the year went on I seem to remember some relaxation of the blackout restrictions. Something happened, as with two lifelong friends we were able to contemplate a camping holiday. We decided to have a week camping at Springhill Farm, a noted beauty spot in Whitwick, now sadly no more. We were to be joined by my nephew, Michael, and Terry's nephew, Freddy, both about ten years old. George, our other companion, lived with his mother who had a small grocers and sweet shop in Hugglescote. It had been our intention to hire a tent from Owens in Coalville but he had none left. Help was to hand from another source. A friend of my late father heard of our plight. Eric Findlay of Fairfield Road, with Tom Ward, coal merchant from Ellistown, supplied the bell tent we used. They took us to Spring Hill in the coal lorry, erected the tent and left us to it.

We had a great time rock climbing and just being under canvas. Meals were rather scratch affairs until Terry's mum and dad came to see us and somehow she cooked us egg and chips on the camp fire. It was ambrosia and the best meal we had that week. At the end of the week we struck camp and went home. The tent hire was twenty Players cigarettes. Such people don't seem to be about today.

As we grew older, our awareness of the war became greater. News was more encouraging as we enjoyed more success on all fronts. 1945 came and we really had the war elsewhere brought home to us when the Allied Forces reached the Concentration Camps and released the unfortunate people who had been imprisoned and tortured there. The news was even more graphic and horrifying when we saw the newsreels.

In April, I registered for National Service and was soon trotting down to Ulverscroft Road, Leicester for my army medical. I am convinced that the criteria was if you were warm you were in. People were beginning to look forward. The war in Europe finally came to an end. We were given a day off and were in our usual haunt, the brook, when the church bells started ringing again and the parties started. We still had to sort out the Japs. As things began to look better, the Leicester work force voted to change their annual holidays from August Bank holiday week to the first week in July. As I worked in Leicester, this applied to me. My father's sister lived in London and invited me to spend the holiday with her. For the first time I saw what the war had done to our great capital. Much of the devastation had been tidied up but bomb sites covered acres. I had spent a month in London in the summer of 1938 and many of the places I had visited were gone. My 1938 tour had been comprehensive, as my uncle was a native, and spent the whole week showing me the sights. Many historic places had gone and I remember particularly the statues of Gog and Magog outside the Guildhall had gone and the Mint standing in isolation on an immense bomb site.

There were lighter sides and I saw John Mills, in a play by his wife, from the gods for two shillings and Lilac Time in the Finsbury Park Open Air Theatre. The latter is still going in the summer, weather permitting. One thing I do wonder is

Iris Gleeson (nee Storer) and the Ace Concert Party. Ibstock W.M.C. 1945 (see page 31)
Back row L to R standing: Fred Storer, Alex Costello, Archie Bott, George Broughton
Front row L to R seated: Doreen Morris, June Edwards, Betty Morris, Vera Bott, Iris Storer, Chesney Deacon

Mrs Kathleen Woodford nee Hunt. (see page 61)

A salvaged letter (see page 73)

SAM AT WORK

The Girl You Left Behind

After his arrival in New York City, cigar-chewing Sam Levy, a steerage passenger from eastern Europe, used to live on the lower East Side not far from the Bowery. Soon he was able to move to upper Broadway. When President Roosevelt took those steps short of war, Sam had already leased a ten room apartment on Riverside Drive.

Slick-haired home-front warrior Mordecai Ezekiel, boss of a government department in Washington, saw to it that his chum Sam would be on the earning end of the war. Rich profits on war contracts let Sam climb up the social ladder, taking two steps at one time. He is now residing in a duplex de luxe apartment on swanky Park Avenue.

Why shouldn't Sam invite beautiful Joan Hopkins, his private secretary, former 5 & 10 cts. salesgirl, up to his place to have dinner with him and cocktails.

Joan is feeling so lonely anyway. More than two years ago, Bob Harrison, the man she wanted to marry, had to leave her for the battlefields of Europe, thousands of miles away.

He is fighting there for Sam Levy and his kind.

Joan is hoping that Bob will return to her safe and sound. But she knows that many of her girl friends are already waiting in vain for their men to return.

Sam knows her predicament and he is trying his darnedest to cheer her up.

Why, Bob wouldn't know it anyway!
And what's a little kiss among friends?

Look for the other pictures of this series.

German anti-Semitic propaganda (see page 79)

the Yanks are "lease-lending" your women. Their pockets full of cash and no work to do, the boys from overseas are having the time of their lives in Merry Old England.

And what young woman, single or married, could resist such "handsome brute from the wide open spaces" to have dinner with, a cocktail at some night-club, and afterwards......

Anyway, so numerous have become the scandals that all England is talking about them now.

While you are away,

Too bad if it should hit you in the last minute.

German anti-American propaganda (see page 79)

Geoff Duckworth liberating an easy chair. (see page 79)

how the population endured the constant bombing and survived. I returned home to find the buses were on strike and finished my journey on the train.

The war in the Far East continued until we heard about the dropping of atomic bombs on the Japanese cities. This lead to the final surrender to General MacArthur. Once again another holiday spent down the brook. More street parties and celebrations.

In the meantime another bomb dropped. The brown envelope with OHMS on it had arrived. It contained a postal order for six shillings advance of pay and a railway warrant for August 16th 1945 to the New Barracks in Lincoln. I went off with my little suitcase and joined a several times failed medical student on the train at Leicester Station. He smoked my last cigarette and after we got there I don't think I saw him again. So started the next phase of my life....... but that's another story!

Frank Gregory

My Personal Wartime Memories

The war years sliced through most of my schooldays. From infant through to junior and, finally, some of my senior school years.

We were lucky, grown-ups said, with bombing and the likes. There were a couple of scares, when four whistling bombs landed two fields away from my home in Ibstock. Massive craters steamed for days afterwards. They became a focal point for many a Sunday morning walk.

I was just seven years old when war was declared. Our crackly old wireless set with the big batteries and valves that glowed in the dark became suddenly important. I could not understand all the fuss the grown-ups made. I still had to go to school, though, walking over a mile across the fields.

The men put air raid sirens high up on several important buildings. I was fascinated watching them sprout on schools, chapels and factory roofs. We did not hang about when they started wailing their stark warning. We were ushered down the nearest dank, foul-smelling shelter. Or if I was at home in bed during an air raid, my only option was to stick my head under the blankets - well, actually they were incredibly heavy old army greatcoats that must have come from the First World War.

In 1940 with the war in full swing, I left the infant school and moved to Ibstock Junior, walking over a mile across fields in my dinner hour. Sometimes the warning sirens would sound on my way home. My other grand-parents, Grandma and Grandad Gregory - he had one leg - who lived at the bottom of Gladstone

Street, would ambush me and apply heaps of delicious jam-layer pudding inside me. It almost made the aid raids seem worthwhile.

Where I lived, at the bottom of Overton Road, it was the training ground for the Home Guard. They came on a Sunday morning, faces blackened and twigs stuck in their helmets. They crawled all over our garden, flattening flowers, cadging mugs of tea, splashing through my favourite fishing haunt, bayoneted rifles held high overhead.

After they had finished manoeuvers, it was the signal for us kids to scour the fields, picking up dummy hand grenades, spent blank bullets and burnt-out flares - like nowadays you might pick up spent fireworks after Bonfire Night. I seem to remember the bombers dropping millions of aluminium strips used to foil enemy planes' tracking signals.

"Put that light out!" became the catch phase during blackout hours. We had to ensure not a crack of light escaped into the night air for fear of attracting German bombing raids. Vehicle headlights were shrouded with black covers with tiny slits. Petrol was rationed, so only cars on priority duties hit the road.

As our house did not have an electricity supply until after the war, escaping light was no bother. We had only very weak oil lamps and candles. During air raids the night skies were criss-crossed with search lights. It was otherwise pitch black, no street lamps. So, to get home we followed the long dry-stone wall down Overton Road just by touch - but where the wall ended we still had a long way to go.

People believed Overton Road was haunted. The ghost, they say, was that of a young wife who, in 1683, was publicly burnt at the stake for poisoning her husband. Legend says this terrible sentence was carried out at the corner of Church End and what is now High Street. Thomas Ridgway, an Ibstock tailor by trade, married the daughter of a Mr Husbands. When the murder was discovered she was seized and sentenced by a judge to be burnt. I confess I have never seen her ghost.

1943 saw me moving to Broom Leys Technical Secondary School, by which time I was convinced the war would go on forever. Children came to know nothing else but war. Holidays did not exist - I was 15 years old before I ever saw the sea.

As Grandad worked at Lodge Farm I was lucky, with food being rationed. Free eggs and milk; a joint of cured pork hanging from the beamed ceiling of our living room. Hens and rabbits supplemented our meals. It was difficult for families to eat a balanced diet on ration books. The shopkeeper had to cut coupons out with scissors - a quarter pound of this, two ounces of that. Sweets were a luxury and bananas non-existent, as were all imported fruits we take for granted today.

Posters warned from shop windows; "Beware - careless talk costs lives!" Every day world news brought tidings of enemy and ally planes shot down. I remember being astounded by the high casualties.

There was a craze for making cigarette lighters out of brass rifle bullet cases. Tank shells were ideal fur cutting down into ashtrays. Almost everybody seemed to smoke, with all the uncertainty - some tobacco smelt like dung, if you know what that smells like!

Kale cutting at Lodge Farm added cow fodder as one of my strangest supplementary diets. We would eat raw sugar beet, mangolds and turnips, then take some home for the rabbit stew. The farmer, who obviously thought we were too greedy, had his own back by giving me and my mate a few roots of horse radish, freshly dug. We chewed the strange root - and our mouths were on fire for two days! That farmer was Jimmy Crane of Lodge Farm, Ibstock. He had a glass eye, as a result of the Boer War - he nearly lost it again that day with laughing! Yes, we enjoyed a sense of humour during that terrible war - much to Adolph Hitler's downfall.

One of the trickiest manoeuvers on a dark, moonless night, was paying a visit to the dry-pan lavatory situated at the very bottom of our long garden. During the blackout you often landed up in the gooseberry bushes.

The thing I hated most was gas mask practice at school. Feeling my lungs would burst, the sweat would pour out, leaving me convinced I was suffocating.

When the final all clear sounded, we learned to live all over again in well-lit streets, without sirens. No more dashing down smelly dugouts. We tasted bananas, visited the seaside - for me, the first time in my life. Best of all, I could welcome back those who had marched halfway across the world to serve our country. Unfortunately, many never returned.

Kenneth M Butcher

Memories From World War Two

As a youth in 1939-45 my lasting memories are:

Two noises which still send a cold shiver down my spine: A siren, especially a wailing siren, even a recording, as it meant a reluctant move under the stairs or out in the cold to the air raid shelter; the change of tone of aircraft engines. German aircraft desynchronised their multi-engines to avoid detection by British aircraft. This resulted in a continuous "up and down" tone.

The orange glow in the low sky on the evening of the German raid on Coventry. The distant noise of anti-aircraft guns and the wreckage of three German aircraft which had crashed nearby as a result of being hit. And I never did see The Wizard of Oz as my parents forbade any visit to the "flicks" until things calmed down.

After the city of Coventry had been reopened, a friend and I cycled to that city some six weeks afterwards and saw the skeletons of previously beautiful buildings and the piled rubble in the ruins of the cathedral.

The railways in war time. The broken windows of carriages from London as they passed through Loughborough station... the alert reaction from railwaymen if a camera was produced (it was illegal to photograph railway subjects)... the frequent notices IS YOUR JOURNEY REALLY NECESSARY... dim carriages full of men in uniform, heavy kitbags which inadvertently, hit you as they were being lifted to the luggage rack... CARELESS TALK COSTS LIVES... notices informing that trespassers were liable to be "shot on sight".

My visit to London in 1942 and my surprise at finding the bus crews were on strike for more money... the remaining buses were driven by soldiers... the conductor-soldier bringing round his bowl and asking for fares "what you think is right"... chains across the open doorway as we passed through the Woolwich docks to see the many ships.

The utmost relief when VE Day arrived, although expected, the *official* announcement on the radio... no more air raids... burn those blackout curtains!... celebrating on the street corner when rations were shared and a bonfire burned in the middle of the road... the hokey-cokey round the bonfire...the chanting of "ten green bottles" which became more slurred as the evening extended... the children's parties in the street with sparse rations being liberally supplied.

Short-changed

Meat was on coupons then

so Mother prevaricated and I

wheedled one more for family lunch.

Fresh sheets for the spare bed and extra milk

counted less than would the joint go round?

We could see each other only at weekends.

Unless there was enough meat on the Sunday roast

even love was rationed.

Heather Chandler

Mrs. M. Booton

My youngest brother went into the navy when he was seventeen. Thank goodness he came home safely. He married a Wren. He is the only brother I have alive out of nine children.

I had just started to work at the Wolsey factory at Coalville. That closed and I then went to work in a munitions factory in Leicester. A fortnight on days and a fortnight on nights. I vividly remember riding on the old trams from the Clock Tower to Macdonald Road, Belgrave. One thing the war did was to seek out women who lived in service. My eldest sister lived in service at Ravenstone Almshouses for five shillings a week. She had to leave and go to work in a munitions factory at Coalville where the Springboard Centre now is. My second eldest sister worked at the Kings Arms pub at Ravenstone for years. She had to leave there and go to work in a large house at Ravenstone that had evacuees.

During the blackout all windows had to be blacked out. Street patrols would knock on your door even if there was only a tiny bit of light showing down the side of your windows.

We were all on clothes coupons which were issued once a year. When the American servicemen came over, white nylon parachutes could be got. My sister-in-law used to make beautiful underwear out of it. Stockings were on coupons so most of the time we went bare-legged, drawing a seam down the back of our legs with a brown pencil to look like the seam of your stockings.

Mrs Kathleen Woodford nee Hunt

Farming

Within minutes of Prime Minister Neville Chamberlain's radio announcement that this country was at war with Germany the stomach-churning wail of the air raid siren sounded across the homes of Coalville. There was silence from the street outside, no evidence of panic. My father, a First World War veteran, was seated across the room, deep in thought. The siren moaned on. It was unreal. Then the tone became a constant one. The "all clear". No bombs would fall on us that day. It had been a practice run.

I was a pupil at Broomleys School and fourteen years old. The government began issuing gas masks, fearing poison gas attacks. Everyone, children and adults, had to walk to Coalville Baths in Avenue Road and, if I recall correctly, the Technical College to be fitted. The masks were horrible things. Thick, smelly rubber, a plastic window which steamed up, a heavy metal air filter with the whole thing clasped tightly over the face with head straps. From that moment everyone had to carry their gas mask at all times - always in a cardboard box. The simplest way was to thread strong string through the box and over the shoulder but most folk made a cover of some sort. At Broomleys the girls were given blue coloured cloth to make the box covers which at least looked a little better. Woe betide the pupil who forgot their gas mask!

Through the war years we lived on London Road next to the old cemetery (parents, two sisters and brother) where, like everyone else, we became used to no street lights, houses in darkness (the Miss Hoskins would quickly be knocking to "put that light out" if the tiniest sliver of light was allowed through heavily shrouded windows), what very few vehicles were about had the dimmest of lamps. All in all, the blackout.

It was a bit special when one evening my sister and I were allowed to go to the pictures - The Regal, I think it was. During the programme - a B picture, a cartoon, Pathe News, trailers and then the "big" picture, an air raid alert was sounded and everyone had to leave! It was the law, but whether money was refunded I cannot recall. Anyway, two teenage girls had more to bother about just then, like getting home in the blackout with enemy bombers droning overhead.

Anyone who has not experienced blackout conditions cannot imagine how totally black it was outside the cinema, which itself showed no lights. Even the stars were hidden that night and we had only a tiny torch to navigate by, a torch with no reflector and the light aperture the size of a modern five pence piece. Anyway, the two of us stumbled and fumbled our way along until, along London Road, things went all wrong! Our way was suddenly blocked by high hedges whichever way we turned. Another squadron of bombers boomed above us but that did not bother us. Being trapped in the total blackness did! We did get out eventually and next day realised we'd wandered off the footpath, through a gap in the privet hedge, and into the front garden of Dr Hamilton's home.

Then came the night of more air activity than usual. The sky to the south glowed a savage red. Coventry was being blitzed. In bed but not sleeping, we all leapt up to the scream of falling bombs. We didn't actually KNOW it was falling bombs, but right then we were not in the mood for debate. In seconds we were downstairs, children under the stairs, Mum and Dad under the dining table just as the explosion came. Homes a hundred yards along London Road were blown up. Little was ever reported about the incident but opinion seemed to go for the story of a bomber jettisoning its deadly cargo when pursued by a Spitfire. It was nothing compared to events in Coventry, but for many a while we were not the only ones to sleep downstairs.

December 1941 brought conscription for women and some months later I had to choose between the ATS, WAAF, WRNS or Women's Land Army. I decided on the latter. I was seventeen years old. Little did I realise it was the start of a lifetime connected with farming. It was a different world at the farm in Shepshed where I was directed for training. Up early to start milking, by hand of course, before breakfast at 7 am followed by mucking-out cow sheds, stables and pig sties using big, heavy shovels and even bigger, heavier wheelbarrows to be staggered with to a distant unlovely steaming pile. It was back breaking work. Afternoons were spent stacking straw, slicing beet or hoeing row upon row of cabbages until it was milking time again before hopefully finishing by 5.30 pm.

No one complained of the hard work, nor indeed of the two pounds a week pay, but it was not a happy time. Other girls were brought in daily from the Ashby camp but I lived-in at the farmhouse where I was not allowed into any rooms other than the kitchen and my small bedroom. Never was there any friendly contact with the family and we had a miserable farm manager to oversee us. The minute my six weeks training period finished, I was off.

Not put off by all that, and anyway, there was a war on, I found myself at Agar Nook, Greenhill. How that came about is another story in itself. From his Forest Road bakery Mr Jack Smith had delivered bread straight from the oven to our family for many years. Hearing I was awaiting another "posting" he suggested visiting Mrs Woodford at Agar Nook. "She wants someone to help her son Eric, who runs the farm since his father died," he said. So I did as he suggested and was given the job. This was accepted by Land Army authorities which meant not going into camp as other girls had to do and having the luxury of still living at home.

The days and the work were equally long and tiring but there was a very different atmosphere from that of my previous place. My job was to take care of all the dairy work. Not a task conjured by the chocolate-box picture of a dainty bonneted maiden surrounded by spring flowers, but one which, for starters, meant not shrieking for help or fainting in a heap as thirty odd cows surged around you, looking like a cattle stampede in one of those Gene Autrey films. Morning milking was followed by bottling-up ready for the daily delivery in Coalville and to do that I had to learn to drive the elderly Morris Oxford, a big, squarely built car used to tow a trailer. Sufficient petrol was allowed for the milk round only. Park Road, High Street, cottages in Lashmore's Yard, Marshall's Row, Stocks's fish shop, Star Tea and Home and Colonial were some of the calls.

The introduction of British Double Summer Time meant work outside could continue until near midnight, but oh, how quickly 5 am next morning came round. Horses were the motive power for everything; ploughing, hay and corn cutting and so on at a time when the old style, even then, method of sowing seed by means of a "fiddle" was still in use. Many's the long day Eric spent walking up and down fields in this way, the fiddle-like box on one shoulder and sawing away with the "bow" which let out the seed to scatter on the ground.

Agar Nook kept three horses and meeting them in the stable for the first time was another daunting experience. It was bad enough putting up forkfuls of hay into high mangers, but pushing past the horses needed some determination. Bonnie, the Shire mare, was the biggest, her powerful frame towering over my frail five-foot-something which was trying to avoid being trampled on by her enormous hooves. But Bonnie was a gentle, quiet creature, always good natured and willing to work.

Working one hundred acres of mixed arable crops along with the dairy herd was as much as the two of us could cope with. Extra help was always very welcome. All Coalville's policemen came to help, particularly at hay-making, and there were always the miners, a grand lot they were, who would just turn up at any time to lend a hand with the heavy work. Names may have been forgotten but not their good-hearted friendship. Occasionally Army lorries would rumble up the drive with German or Italian prisoners of war from Ashby to work in the fields. I had little contact with them but, older men, they worked hard while waiting for the end of a war they had not wanted.

So that was my wartime work, like so many other women doing jobs which had always been done by men. I had wanted to join the WAAF but it was an ambition firmly overruled by mother. The war began while I was still fourteen and at school. It ended when I was twenty in 1945, the same year I changed my name. Yes, Eric and I were married at Coalville Parish Church, a marriage which gave us forty seven wonderful years together.

POSTSCRIPT: Look now and you will find no trace of Agar Nook Farm today. Even Bardon Hill itself, on whose slopes we farmed, is hardly recognisable. The fields we ploughed and sowed are all beneath a housing estate, but many happy memories still crowd around. The junction of Kenmore Crescent with Greenhill Road marks where the white farm gate once stood, a gate opened so nervously for the first time by a teenage girl so long ago.

Edna Dorothy Smith nee Storer

I was still at school when the war started and I can remember going to school with my gas mask. You had to carry it at all times. We had lessons at school on how to put them on and we had to wear them for short periods to get used to them.

I left school a few months after the war started. I was then fourteen years old. I worked in the hosiery in Earl Shilton until I was seventeen and then I was old enough to do war work. I got a job at Desford Aerodrome where repairs were done on Defiants and Mitchell bombers. I was sent from the aerodrome to a school in Leicester to learn all about the job. I was at this school for two months and we were taught all about the planes and how they worked. At the end of the two months we were then set an exam and I am proud to say I passed top of the class. It was so interesting. I then went back to the aerodrome. When I first went back, I worked on the fire extinguisher system on the Defiants. I worked with an

Irish man called Paddy who was very funny. He was cross-eyed but he taught me a lot.

Because I had passed out top of the class in Leicester, when there was a vacancy for a better job, I was offered it. I then went to the other side of the aerodrome to be on the Flight Gang for Defiants and Mitchell bombers. There were six of us on the flight gang, three men and three girls, and we all got on very well together.

When the AA pilots brought the planes down, the flight gang were the first to board the planes to check everything. When we got to know the pilots, they would sometimes bring us little gifts, like boxes of kippers from Yarmouth and chocolates when they could get them. There were women AA pilots and they sometimes used to bring make-up for us girls and once I remember they brought my friend Doris and me a pair of nylons each, which were almost impossible to get during the war.

When the planes had been repaired and inspected and passed, the AA pilots came to take them away and the Defiants, being small planes, four of the flight gang had to sit on the tail plane while the pilot revved the plane up. I only sat on the tail plane once. I was only four foot ten inches, and very slim. The airstream blew me off and across the aerodrome. It was so funny. It blew all the hairgrips out of my hair and there I lay on the airfield. My workmates came and picked me up, none the worse for my experience, but after that the others sat on the tailplane and I stood at the front of the aircraft where the pilot could see me, and he signalled to me when he had enough revs, and then I would signal to my workmates to jump off the tailplane so that the plane could taxi down the airfield.

When it was foggy and the planes could neither land or take off, there was nothing for the flight gang to do, so we would take a pack of cards into a Mitchell bomber and play until the weather got better.

It wasn't all work and no play though during the war. Another hangar housed Tiger Moths, and there the young men were taught how to fly. I met one of these young men called Dave, and I went out with him all the time he was there. He would circle round the airfield before take off. I wore a red silk scarf round my neck so that he could pick me out and he would come and kiss me before take off. We didn't realise we could be seen from the offices. Major Read, who was the boss, sent for me to go to his office. He was very nice and told me he thought it was very romantic, and to move away from the offices and continue to have my kiss. It was just jealous fuddy-duddies in the offices who had complained.

The airmen would organise dances at the officers mess at the aerodrome and the girls from the nearby villages would go. We had some smashing times.

After the training at Desford Aerodrome, the young men were sent to Africa to finish their training. They went by ship out there and of course they couldn't tell us the name of the ship. I didn't hear from Dave. Quite a while later, I heard he had gone down with the ship when it was torpedoed. It was very sad at the time and it took me a long time to get over it.

Marjorie Joyce Jones

When the Second World War started in 1939, I was living in Nottingham. I was working with a firm called Wallace Kings off Drury Hill. This was a quaint part of Nottingham bordered with lots of small shops. Caves ran underneath and down to the bottom of the hill. Some of these were excavated to use in the event of air raids. We were advised to bring a tin of biscuits in case we were down there for any length of time. It was surprising how cool and fresh it was below ground.

We were issued with gas masks which we carried to and fro from work, together with torches which we were allowed to use in the blackout. The blitz of Nottingham was frightening. Mother and I sheltered in the pantry. That was considered to be the safest place, under the stairs. We listened with thumping hearts as the bombs came whistling down. All the windows were blown out. After the all clear, people picked their way over the rubble to view the damage. After seeing the huge craters all around our houses, we marvelled that we were still alive. Whole streets had disappeared. We gasped at the devastation of one night's work. People were walking around in their night clothes, too shocked to care.

Being twenty years old, I was to be in the first age group to be called up for war work. My friend's father was working in Bottesford, near Grantham. An aerodrome was being built there. They were erecting hangar huts, which were oblong in shape, and Nissen huts - rounded with corrugated metal roofs. These were in readiness for the Air Force. The London firm of C & T Painters anticipated employing women. We acquired a green card and went to see the boss (Gus). So we got our own war job. We bought bib and brace overalls from B H Stores with a few of our precious clothing coupons.

We set off each morning at 6.30 to catch a ramshackle old Skills bus without a door. The aerodrome was nine miles round. We headed for the communal site where we met the boss. We were given instructions. We pasted two inch wide strips over all the plasterboard seams in the huts. They were then ready for painting. We were all handy with scissors and found the work interesting and loved it.

The only drawback was the lack of toilet facilities. The one we knew of was a chemical one in the communal hut where the boss hung out. However, we came across a farm house. We asked permission to use theirs on payment of a small fee each time. They were most obliging and brought hot water and soap and towel. This toilet wasn't always convenient as we worked in different places. The boss gave us a key to a building where we could change our clothes, this after I had my skirt stolen. Whilst working near here we compromised by using a bucket.

We walked along the lanes carrying paint pots, singing as we went, flicking pebbles off our scrapers. We were happy the war seemed a long way off. The boys in the officers' mess supplied us with water for our tea. Sometimes we were given pudding and custard and, if lucky, cake. There were a number of Irish working there. We chatted as we waited in the cocoa queue. A man had a stove outside for this purpose. Sometimes we bought small cakes - luxury indeed!

Gus had a foreman called Douglas. He was a Welshman with blue eyes that twinkled and laughed. After some time he left to join the navy. He and I corresponded.

The inside work was finished. The aerodrome was working in full swing. We painted sashes on taller buildings. We got used to climbing ladders like monkeys. We endured lots of cheeky remarks such as "Are you putting that paint on the right way up?" etc. Sadly the work here was finished.

So it was back to the Labour Exchange and on to pastures new. Our next venture was a munition factory at Colwick. There they made torpedo rockets. I worked a paint sprayer back and forth. It painted the insides of four foot long tubes, after which they travelled through big hot ovens. When they reached the other side, they were varnished. When we used the toilets, we had to clock in and out. We worked one week days and one week nights. The work quickened up and got harder as we were pressed to beat the target all the time. At the end of the day, I ached in every bone. It was terrible trying to sleep during the day. You were disturbed by the sounds of the baker, milkman and children going to school. It disrupted your eating habits. You often got up for snacks during the night. They played the record of Bing's White Christmas over and over on the night shift. How we wished summer would come!

Saturdays we went to the pictures. We queued to see Deanna Durban and Dorothy Lamour etc. Coming off nights we had trouble keeping awake. During day shifts, we had "Music while you work" in the canteen. It was good entertainment.

We were eventually moved again to a place making carburettors. There I went to school for two days, learning to read a micrometer. It was a restful change with nothing heavier than a pencil to lift. This work was lighter but the hours were long. I worked a drilling machine and another one making jet boxes.

The war had gone on for almost six years. Christmas 1944, we decorated the machines with aluminium waste. It shone and sparkled like tinsel. People were moving on gradually. I went back to being a sewing machinist, making babies frocks. Douglas came home safe and sound and in September 1945 we were married. A month afterward he was demobbed. Later we adopted two babies. We had forty seven years of happy marriage.

Years later our eldest daughter went to live in Shardlow. We moved to Castle Donington in 1980. Here I shall stay until I get my final call-up.

Marjorie E Woods

I was born in Coalville, and apart from a few years in Ravenstone, I have lived here all of my life. We moved back here when I was seven, and until I was eleven, I was educated at Belvoir Road School. In 1935 I went to Broomleys School, which was very convenient, as by then we were living in Meadow Lane. It was in 1939 (that fateful year!) that I left school to start work in the office of the Leicestershire Coal Sales Association, which dealt with all the pits in the district - Desford, Ellistown, Nailstone, New Lount, Snibston, South Leicester and Whitwick - plus, later on, the opencast mines.

The offices were in spacious accommodation above the Midland Bank, right opposite the Station. I believe the old Bank building was one of the most attractive buildings in the town and I have always regretted that it was demolished when the Precinct was built. The Boardroom, on the first floor, was a magnificent room with fireplaces at each end, and large windows. The massive table was always beautifully polished, with fine comfortable chairs on either side and at each end. All the colliery managers came there regularly for meetings, at which I was expected to serve tea and biscuits - a rather daunting task at first, for a new girl to serve all those important gentlemen. One thing I never understood was that right through the war, in spite of food shortages, we were never without a tin of very good biscuits!

Mr Charles W Ashton was the office chief - a major in the First World War - and he took a great interest in organising anything which would help the war effort. As the need for blood escalated, he was instrumental in helping the National Blood Transfusion Service, and regular sessions were held at the collieries. I frequently went to the local colliery offices with correspondence regarding these sessions, which were well supported by the miners. It was by delivering letters to the Snibston office that I first met Les Woods, who was to become my husband! I had seen him at Broomleys School, but as he was then a 4th year, and I a lowly 1st year, our paths never crossed! Anyway, after one or two more visits to Snibston regarding blood transfusions, Les finally called me at the office to arrange our first date. After consultation with my parents, and they deciding that he was a suitable young man to date their only child, we started to meet - but at first, only once a week! That was in 1940, and in 1941 Les was called into the Army - to the Royal Artillery, based in Edinburgh - which seemed a very long way from Coalville!

It was at Redford Barracks that Les trained as a signaller. Having been Assistant Scoutmaster in Hugglescote Robin Hood Scouts, he was familiar with Morse Code, so found he was conversant with signals. Soon afterwards, a notice appeared on the Board, asking for volunteers for a Special Service Brigade - an extra six shillings and eightpence a day, and civilian billets! Les volunteered, and went to Dumbarton, into a pleasant household and then started his real training at Achnacarry Castle - and found himself in No 6 Commando! Thus began the real war, so far as I was concerned! Commando life was, to say the least, pretty precarious!

Meanwhile, back home in Coalville, I was continuing my clerical education at the Technical College. I would cycle from Broomleys where I was living with my parents - there were no street lamps and cycle lamps were shielded so that only a minimum gleam could be seen. This protected us, hopefully, from being seen from enemy aircraft. The road was much less populated in those days, yet cycling through the dark nights, by the spinney and open fields opposite the school, I don't ever remember being afraid. One night, going from College, walking along Belvoir Road with my friend, Eileen Wileman, to stay the night at her parents' home, we were passing the old Police Station (now the Magistrates Courts) when the air raid siren on the building started up. A most peculiar thing happened to both of us - we were almost thrown sideways. I never understood what could have caused this, though it was a dreadfully loud noise, but as we recovered we roared with laughter.

We were told that the space below a flight of stairs could be the safest place to shelter - apart from a direct hit by a bomb. In Meadow Lane, we had a storeroom beneath our stairs and it had a door opening on to the backyard. In a raid my parents would go in there and make themselves comfortable on deck chairs. On the night that Leicester had its big raid, I was out with Les, and he took me to his home, as his mother was alone. His father, Percy Woods, was an officer in the Home Guard and his sister was with the VAD nurses - both on stand-by duty. My parents were worried about my absence, but when I returned home it was to hear the story that my mother had dozed off to sleep and had suddenly woken up saying, "Jim, we've been gassed!" Dad thought that was ridiculous and Mum must have been dreaming. However, she insisted, and then they discovered she had leant against a sack of onions which Dad had stored in the outhouse. Apparently one of the pamphlets mother had read stated that one type of gas had an onion smell!

Earlier in the war we had seen the evacuees arrive from London and Birmingham. Some came from very well-to-do homes, and seemed to be placed in similar types of home here. Others went to less well-to-do families. Some stayed on quite happily and fitted in well with their host families - and others were not so happy. Gradually, quite a lot of children drifted back to their homes, but some stayed on until the air raids stopped. Many still keep in touch with their host families.

Mr Ashton's daughter, Cynthia, was secretary of the Red Cross Penny-a-week Fund, and my mother and I were collectors in part of Broomleys. Cynthia joined the ATS and Mr Ashton suggested that I take over the secretaryship. Being unable to do a great deal to help the war effort, apart from knitting "comforts" for the forces (scarves, socks etc) and writing masses of letters to Les and my cousins in the Forces, I agreed. My friend, Mary Oakford (now Barnett) agreed to become joint secretary with me. Each month we were able to use a room at the office, to receive and empty the collection boxes from the collectors throughout the Urban District. I wish I had kept account of the total money collected - almost all of it in pennies, but some silver too. I saved the envelopes from the office post, and we used those to pack the money. to take to the Co-operative Bank in Marlborough Square. These were *old* pennies and quite weighty, compared with our tiny pennies of today, and very heavy the collections were to carry. It was gratifying to learn from returned prisoners of war, how much they appreciated the few comforts which they had received from the Red Cross!

Never will I forget D Day!! I arrived at the office that morning having not heard the preliminary report on the radio. The office staff were strangely quiet. Soon after I arrived the caretaker, Mrs Gaskin, came down from her top floor flat, to tell me there was to be an important announcement, and would I like to hear it. With permission from Mr Ashton, I went upstairs and heard about the landings in France. At once, I realised Les was there in the first wave of troops. because there had been no letters for some days. As I left the flat, I was aware of the sun streaming through a skylight above the staircase and dear Mrs Gaskin leaning over the stair-rail and saying to me, "I feel so sorry for you, my love." Mr Ashton came to me and asked if I would like to go home but I told him I wished to work as usual. It was a very strange and fearful time for Les's family and for me - by this time we had been married just seven months - and it was three weeks before I received a tiny card sayiing he was safe. During the first days after D Day, friends and acquaintances would stop to chat and ask whether I had heard from Les. By the end of the second week, I found people were avoiding me - obviously afraid to ask. In September the Commandos returned, to prepare for action elsewhere, but Les had injured his shoulder and went to hospital in Wales.

He had also served in the landings in Algiers, but spoke little about his experiences in either war zone. I have only learned of some of the events from books, and from memoirs he wrote during the months before he died, in September 1994.

That was my wartime, with many happy memories and many sad ones. My father became steward of the Constitutional Club in Coalville, and Les and I lived there after he was demobbed. We made a home of two rooms on the top floor until we could find a home of our own. Our daughter, Susan, was born in 1947, at Market Bosworth and we bought our first house (in Greenfields Drive) in January 1948. Our son, Nigel, came along in 1952 - our family complete! We had a very happy marriage - over fifty years. Did our wartime experiences, our separations and worries help to cement our union? I'm sure they did.

Mrs F M Davies

When I was twenty one, I became engaged to a boy from Coalville. I met him at Coalville Grammar School in Forest Road. We left there in 1935 and during the next few years we had such lovely times. He learned to fly at Desford Aerodrome, along with several local boys, including two of the Ball brothers, Les and Pete. They loved flying and as the war years rolled along they became attached to RAFVR and were called up a month or two before the imminent war. They trained together then at various aerodromes, Sywell (Northants), Arbroath, Montrose and Lossiemouth and had a spell billeted in Trinity College, Cambridge.

Somewhere at the end of these courses, they had to choose - fighters or bombers. Jim chose bombers and eventually piloted Wellingtons from an additional aerodrome on Newmarket racecourse. His machine was B for Bertie. The people of Newmarket were marvellous to all the air crews stationed there. I holidayed there a couple of times staying at the White Lion, where we were treated royally. I then met all his crew and what grand chaps they all were. One afternoon when they were not flying, there was racing on the other heath and they all sauntered over and watched Gordon Richards win the Cesarewitch!

One night after a raid, they ran into an electrical storm over the channel - instruments blown haywire and not knowing to which land they were heading. Once over land, orders had to be given to bale out. Jim landed with a jolt on the bottom of his back and, when he collected himself, he was on the back gardens of a little row of houses. After being violently sick and feeling awful, he knocked on one door where there was a light. The lady daren't open up as it was pitch dark. She looked through the curtains. He told her who he was and would she just give him a drink of water as he felt so ill. She still dare not open the door but, when she answered him in English, he fainted, so thankful to be in England. The plane crashed on Hampton Court, hurting no-one, and the six crew had all landed within a mile of each other around Hounslow Barracks. The rear gunner,

Ginger, landed in a tree, could not disentangle his 'chute, and just had to hang there. A sentry on duty around the barracks paraded underneath him and Ginger shouted down who he was etc, but the sentry left him for two hours, saying that all the Germans should be where he was, and when the guards changed duties, they decided they'd better do something about him. The first ladder they fetched was reputedly too short - they were gone ages finding another. The only casualty amongst the crew was a broken ankle. Having baled out successfully, they became members of the Caterpillar Club and were presented with a gold caterpillar brooch.

His plane was missing following a raid on Kiel on the night of 24th-25th November 1940 - shot down into the North Sea by flak. Their bodies were never found.

S. G. Redfern

At the going down of the Sun and in the Morning we remember them – I wonder?

Seated in the church at Packington with my wife and other guests at the wedding of a nephew some few years ago and, awaiting the arrival of the bride, my attention was drawn to the board listing the names of the men of the village whose lives were lost in the two World Wars. A great sadness came over me to see once again the name of a great friend, workmate and fellow sportsman, a man who I had played cricket with. As I sat in silence my mind was taken taken back some fifty years or so.

I stood by an opening to a field amid the bustle of war activity in Italy awaiting assistance from a Canadian Tank Unit. We a support group of some twenty vehicles carrying heavy mortars and machine guns. We had driven into this field the previous evening on our way to give support to troops attacking German positions in the hills some ten miles away. Heavy rain had turned the field into a sea of mud during the night and consequently we were bogged down. As we waited, a famous Scottish Battalion marched by and to my delight and amazement I saw my friend marching head and shoulders (he was 6ft 3 or 4 inches tall) above everybody else.

A halt was called and he and I had a chance of a few moments reminiscing and to swop yarns. I was able to supply him with some cigarettes for although he and I were non-smokers he was concerned, as Section Corporal, that his men had no smokes and it gave me great pleasure to see them lighting up - a soldier's small comfort. Shortly afterwards, they continued their march accompanied

by the thunder of noise as American planes passed overhead.Their mission was to soften up the enemy defences prior to a full scale attack.

We watched as bombs were dropped and the planes turned for home. As they passed overhead, we were horrified to see bombs falling on us. Obviously, some of the pilots had decided to jettison their load rather then land with them. With our slit trenches full of water and no cover, we had to lie down in the mud. The explosions caused much damage and mud, water and broken vehicles were flung into the air. Our friends, the Canadians, suffered the most damage and, such was their anger that they opened fire with their Ack-Ack guns. An excitable Italian who had a smattering of English said, "English bombs, Germans duck! German bombs, English duck! American bombs, everybody duck!"

This unfortunate incident caused quite a delay and we were a day late moving up to support our boys in that particular offensive. We were always on the move and on meeting fierce opposition, many good friends were lost. New mates joined us and we suffered hardships never to be forgotten. Hardened as I was, when news from home came some weeks later to tell that my friend had died of wounds sustained in action, I was devastated. Given a brief rest period and pulled out of the line, I was able to visit the hospital in Caserta and was told by the matron that depite all efforts to save him, and just as he was recovering form surgery, he lapsed into a coma and passed away. I was able to visit his grave in a nearby cemetery to pay my respects to a brave man.

The sudden upsurge of organ music heralding the arrival of the bride, brought me out of my reverie and I wondered as I saw the happy couple united in marriage, how different it might have been had it not been for the bravery and sacrifice of thousands of men like my great, quiet, heroic friend, Arthur Spare.

Mrs W. Garner

My boy friend was called up on October 14th 1939 to do his National Service. I went to see him off at Paddington Station, West London, and as we were having our farewell embrace I popped a little "Black Cat" lucky charm into his pocket.

He served his time on various ships including H.M.S. Argonaut. While he was away on Active Service in the Royal Navy, I was on war work at the Concordia Firm of Electrical Cables, Communication & Wiring, East Midlands.

One day, us factory girls were having our lunch time break in the works canteen, listening as we always did to the latest one o'clock news on the radio, when it was announced that HMS Argonaut had been torpedoed off Sardinia whilst on Convoy Duty.

After weeks of anxiety wondering what news I would eventually hear, I received an official letter, with a blue stamp, marked Salvaged from the Sea. Inside was a badly damaged half burned letter from my husband. When I opened the letter much to my surprise and delight, I found inside a very colourful picture of a cheeky sailor with a big grin giving an enthusiastic V for Victory sign.

We have now been married for fifty-four years and we still have the little black cat lucky charm that my husband kept with him during his six years of National Service.

Raymond Wright - Ex Royal Navy Telegraphist

My father was an Ibstock miner who migrated at the turn of the century to the then newly opened Yorkshire mines. All my brothers and sisters were born in Yorkshire. On the death of my father in 1940 I came down here on the border of Leicestershire/South Derbyshire to live, until I was old enough to volunteer for the Forces. This I did in June 1942, joining the Royal Navy as a Wireless Telegraphist. In this capacity I was present in the initial assault on D Day 1944 remaining in the Normandy battle zone until the campaign was over. I also served in the sea-borne assault on Walcheren Island in the Schelde Estuary Holland. On November 1st 1944 I completed my service time minesweeping in the Atlantic off Southern Ireland.

I think that briefly covers my war service, but the story I want to relate concerns a young American paratrooper who was training over here for the assault on D Day. He was my blood cousin, the youngest son of my father's only sister who emigrated to America with her husband who also came from Ibstock. They settled in the mining area of Illinois U.S.A. and had quite a large family.

The young man's name was Private Raymond Ward of the 101st Airborne Division. He spent a leave or furlough, as the Americans called it, with my uncle and aunt Mr & Mrs Arthur Wright of Hall Street Ibstock, who still lived in the house where his mother, Rose Wright, had been born and raised.

During this leave period he was able to visit the Ward side of the family as well as the Wrights who were all very proud to make him welcome. Unfortunately I was unable to meet him as I was also engaged in the training for the Normandy Invasion. Raymond Ward apparently thoroughly enjoyed his stay amongst his English relatives and my aunt told me, after the war, that he'd been more upset at leaving them than her own three sons who were also serving in the Forces. We could only assume that this lad of nineteen years who was truly serving in a high risk organisation must have felt that his chances of survival were not too good, which sadly was only too true for he was badly wounded in the parachute drop over St-Mere-Eglise, Normandy and died of his wounds a few days later, for which he was awarded the Purple Heart.

I went back to Normandy during the 50th Anniversary Celebrations in 1994 and found that the three lads who were killed aboard my landing craft had no known grave. I went to the American Cemetery near St-Laurent-sur-Mer and the American authorities went to a lot of trouble to find my cousin's grave and took my wife and me down in an electrically powered vehicle and took photographs of us standing by the grave. A most moving experience, as all the other graves were marked as 18 and 19 year old boys all around him. When they knew that he was my relative they treated us like royalty and loaded us up with a terrific amount of information and the photograph they'd taken of us at the graves where we had placed flowers.

I have since received a beautiful coloured lithograph of this splendid cemetery with a black and white photograph of his grave set in it. This was sent from Washington DC by the Colonel in charge of the organisation.I have written to thank him and his staff for their kindness.

I would advise anyone with American relatives buried over there to make the pilgrimage and they will be royally treated. I hope to make the same pilgrimage again another year.

R. J. Pickering

I served as a professional in the Royal Navy, specialising in Radio Communications from 1937. Consequently I saw active service from day one of World War II in 1939, participating in Atlantic convoys, Malta convoys, the Greek and Crete campaigns, the Western Desert campaign and finally the D Day landings.

Most of the events of the above have been well documented and chronicled throughout the last fifty years - so I'm going to relate a few encounters and incidents that made a big impression on me at the time, they generally come under the headings of The Good, The Bad And The Ugly.

The Good

After the D Day landings on June 6th 1944 and when the beach-heads were well established - HRH King George VI visited the troops in Normandy, and my ship HMS Garth was instrumental in bringing him back to the UK on "D17" (June 24th 1944). This particular channel crossing was the worst I've ever experienced. I was on the bridge (an open type) with the Captain and HRH. We were all wore oilskins - we had to, for the tremendous twenty feet waves were completely enveloping the ship from from bow to stern as we battled against a terrific head-on sea. The crossing took us approximately four to five hours - including three attempts to enter Dover harbour - there being a serious danger of the ship capsizing with a very important person aboard. Anyway we finally made it on the crest of a wave!

Whilst standing alongside HRH I realised what a "good man" he was - a monarch to proud of and an inspiration to all the armed forces at that fateful time. The same can be said of Field Marshal Lord Montgomery who we took across to the beach-heads. Standing next to him his power and strength of character made me realise the invasion was in good hands and ultimate victory inevitable.

The Bad

During my service with the Mediterranean Fleet I was sent at very short notice into the Western Desert on "special service" to join the Naval Radio Station at the beleaguered garrison at Tobruk. I was there throughout the long siege until it fell after combined artillery, bombing and tank fire on June 20th 1942. Whilst there I met a notorious character by the name of Ronald Chesney. He was an R.N.V.R. Lieutenant in command of a three-masted schooner the Khein-el-dim. He was a giant of a man, standing six feet three, in his seaboots, had the inevitable beard and an ear-ring in his right ear. He was nicknamed the "last of the buccaneers". In fact he was a real piratical character. He had apparently been involved in smuggling and gun running activities on the North African coast before the war and therefore was considered an ideal man to command the requisitioned Egyptian schooners and bring supplies to Tobruk and other beleaguered garrisons on the Western Desert coast. So it proved, for he did a good job in this respect. He'd been selected on the same principle as the "dirty dozen" were selected because of their criminal activities. Make no mistake about it - he was a criminal, having being accused of murdering his grandmother in Scotland at the age of seventeen, although the verdict was not proven.

However, came the day of the capture of Tobruk on June 20th 1942, at 1500 hours. I, incidentally, made the signal on behalf of the 8th Army Staff Officer that General Klapper's 25,000 garrison of mainly South African and Australian troops plus some British Guards Brigades had surrendered. We had to get out fast. I managed to get aboard the minesweeper HMS Aberdare which although repeatedly hit by shell fire and 88mm tank fire, managed to escape under the cover of a smoke screen from an MTB. We picked up what soldiers we could - those who had swum out to us as we left harbour. Chesney and the Khein-el-din however were not so lucky. The schooner received a direct hit and began to sink rapidly. Some of its crew were taken off by an MTB, but Chesney refused to leave. Being true to naval traditions, he was going down with his ship. He was last seen saluting the White Ensign, but apparently as soon as his beard got wet he started swimming for the coast, where he was eventually taken prisoner.

Nothing was heard of him again until after the war when apparently he managed to get a job in the Control Commission in Germany, but after a while his criminal activities once again surfaced. Due to his womanising, gambling, and heavy drinking he was in deep financial trouble. So he returned to the UK to ask his wife and mother-in-law to bail him out, but they refused. So he shot them both and high tailed it back to Germany via the Harwich Ferry, but Interpol had been alerted. They tracked him down in the Black Forest where he shot himself! The end of a very bad lot.

The Ugly

On the 18th March 1941, a beautiful steam yacht SS Rosaura arrived at Tobruk. A really smart one-funnelled vessel, about 2,000 tons, requistioned by the Navy for transport purposes. She came alongside and embarked as many Italian prisoners as she could possibly carry. They were packed down below, on the upper deck and the boat deck. She sailed at 1300 hours on a beautiful sunny afternoon. We watched her sail serenely to the harbour entrance, when suddenly a terrific explosion occurred. She'd hit a mine and blew up. All available small boats immediately headed for the area to pick up what survivors they could, but there was only a very small number. An ugly waste of human life.

Now for a touch of the farcical. Whilst in the desert I was sent to Benghazi for duty in the Radio Station there, but after a while I had to return overland to Tobruk. A thousand or so Italian prisoners of war had to make the same journey in an Australian Army lorry convoy. So I and about half-a-dozen others were issued with 303 rifles (I think we were given some ammunition, but I wouldn't swear to it!) and we were to be the armed guard for these prisoners. Fortunately, they didn't want to escape, otherwise we would have been in dead trouble. We arrived back at Tobruk without mishap.

I served on the following ships:

H.M.S. Furious - Air Craft Carrier, North Atlantic Patrols.

H.M.S. Orion - Cruiser, Greek and Crete evacuations, Malta Convoys etc.

H.M.S. Fame - Destroyer, Atlantic Convoys.

H.M.S. Garth - Destroyer, European operations, D Day, Normandy Landings.

H.M.S. Bicester - Destroyer, Post war operations.

H.M.S. Aberdare - Minesweeper, North African Coast.

H.M.S. Hotspur - Destroyer, Post war operations.

Shore based - Western Desert

Geoff Duckworth

After I had joined the Navy I was stationed down in Portsmouth. One particular night there was an air-raid and being gunnery ratings and being on duty watch we were issued with Lewis guns and the orders were that we were to only fire at the flares coming down. Myself and my oppo positioned ourselves and after a few minutes planes were heard and the flares started dropping. Of course, over the Portsmouth dockyard area there were always barrage balloons.

We received the order to fire and at the same time we noticed that a flare looked as if it was about to drop onto a barrage balloon. We both let fire at this, well I did in particular, anyway. Unfortunately we misjudged the distance of the flare, it must have been falling behind the barrage balloon, so instead of the flare going down, the damn barrage balloon did instead! In flames!

My girlfriend at the time was in the ATS and she was on a gunsight down at Hayling Island, not far from us. The day after the balloon incident I went down to see how she was. She started relating the story about the barrage balloon, and added "I suppose it was one of you damn Navy chaps." I didn't admit it at the time but I expect it was the one that I had had a go at!

By 1943 I had been drafted into Combined Operations. During the landings on Sicily we were working non-stop, night and day, ferrying everything ashore, men, ammunition, rations etc. By the second or third day we got the chance to get ashore. About 400 yards away from our landing beach was an abandoned vineyard. Inside the buildings were the large vats and barrels. You could stand inside them they were so immense! Some of the vats still contained wine that was maturing.

The Germans had been there before us and poisoned the water supplies and so we hadn't got any water. Most of the time in these operations we wore battle-dress rather than Naval uniform and so we were carrying water bottles. We all thought this was the opportunity to have a good drink and fill the water bottles up with this wine, red wine it was. Unfortunately it didn't quench our thirst but we stuck at it and still kept drinking it! We carried on until we felt pretty woozy and tired as well with not having any rest for a couple of days.

My oppo and I were on duty on the beach that night, the Germans would bomb the ships at night, and with our Lewis guns we had to fire at the flares as they came down. After a while, when everything had gone quiet, we decided to get our heads down if we possibly could. We looked around for somewhere and went through a courtyard into a building. We noticed that there were some other chaps in there so we kept quiet and got down and the next thing we knew it was early morning. We woke up and lo and behold, it was full of other chaps all right! They must have been people that had been killed in the initial landing and they had been wrapped up and laid there awaiting burial. We'd been sleeping in a temporary morgue!

In early 1945 our flotilla had been drafted over to Belgium, mainly Ostend, we moved along the coast doing a variety of jobs and when Antwerp and Flushing were liberated we had orders to move to Antwerp. Antwerp had become a vital supply port and from then we followed the army through to the Rhine crossings which we took part in. The first landings that we did were below Arnhem and after this we took part in the second attack of Arnhem.

We'd had a rough time of it generally, once action is engaged you just keep going and going until the position is secured and then you can relax. We eventually got the chance to rest and our officers had been looking around and we had orders, because they felt they needed a bit of a rest, to liberate some easy chairs from a bombed building so that they could relax. Technically this might seem like looting but these buildings on the German side had been obliterated and the chairs were just waiting to be picked up.

F. G. Whittington

I was married at Castle Donington church on December 16th 1939 and became a member of the local fire service. I remember one occasion putting out fire bombs in the field at the rear of where I now live.

I was called up on September 14th 1940 to join the 26th AA Regiment RA stationed at Derby on gun sites in the area. Our commanding officer was Major the Lord Scarsdale of Kedleston Hall. Shortly after, we took up gun sites at Seamington Aerodrome.

A few months later on August 3rd 1941 we were in convoy to the Middle East. After nine weeks at sea, having called at Cape Town, we finally arrived at Port Tuffie the mouth of the Red Sea and into Egypt and a sand storm. After a short stay in the desert we spent the next eighteen months in Palestine, Syria and Cyprus engaged in the defence of Haifa Docks, oil refinery and aerodrome from where allied aircraft used to fly to bomb North Africa.

We were soon to join the 8th Indian Division and arrived in southern Italy to take part in the advance up the Adriatic Coast. We eventually came to a halt and were transferred to the eastern side of Italy to take up positions for the final attack on Monte Cassino. The shelling lasted for four days and four nights during which time we received some German leaflets - toilet use only, I thought.

We travelled north through the mountains and had the misfortune of being blown up by one of the numerous mines while crossing a river bed at Ruffino and we lost one of my detachment before we reached Pisa. Then we crossed westward to Monza and the surrender of the German army.

After four and a half years we returned home for a short leave and then we were sent to Germany for a further six months before demob.

Ditilawa Ceylon 1943

The moon, a silver magnet, drew
Me from my dreams,
And down the night I wandered through
Its silent beams.
I strode the silver streets until
The end of town,
And slowly started up the hill
And there sat down
Beneath a sky of eastern stars;
And heard the thrum
Of distant drums and sad sitars
And sweet, the hum
Of softly singing Sinhalese.
I heard the groan
From far away, the wail, the wheeze,
The gasps, the moan
Of anguish, squeals of wheels in pain
As round the bends
The train from Kandy feels the strain
As it ascends
The hill. The scavengers of dark
Perform their rights,
And snarling pariah dogs that bark
In greedy fights
For carrion from a panther's kill,
And keep at bay
The slobbering jackals that mill
Around and bray
Their insane laughter to the night.
I heard, far off,
The wild hog snort in startled fright
A leopard's cough,
And then the screech owl's eerie scream,
And saw the eyes
Of chital deer in moon light gleam;
And heard the cries

Of jungle cocks disturbed from sleep
By lantern flares
As native trappers gently creep
To lay their snares.
The trees were bright with fire-fly lights
And gliding packs
Of flying foxes flew in flights
Like vampire bats
To feed on fruit. The croaking crake
That tree frog made
Combined with those cicadas make
In forest glade
Pulsated through the air a sound
Of rhythmic throbs.
And boughs began to shake all round
As angry mobs
Of monkeys screamed as one lone bear
In search of bees
Began to prowl and growl too near
Their bed-time trees.
A mongoose hunted near
My feet and tried
To open up my pack and peer
Inside, then spied
My face and stared at me with eyes
So feared by snakes.
He bounded off with peevish cries
Towards the lakes
Below. And I lay back and felt
At peace and sighed
For war to cease. With joy I smelt
On every side
The smells and spells and scents of trees,
The flame-tree's flower,
The fragrant frangipanis
Majestic power.
An old bull elephant trumped loud,
A bugle blew,

The sky became a cloak of cloud,
A wind lashed through
The tall bamboo and rain began
To fall, and ants
Invaded all my clothes and ran
Inside my pants.
The midges stung, mosquitoes bit
My neck and head
My seat became a watery pit,
And leeches bled
My arms and legs. I rose to leave
My forest hide
And with sadness began to weave
And slip and slide
My way below. My heart remained
With all the charms
Of Ceylon's paradise. I'd gained
In Lanka's arms
The peace that calms a soldier's breast.
Where ever ship
May take me now, my heart will rest
In Serendip.

Major John Gillies Shields

Sydney Wallace, S/Sgt. 11409706

I was 32 years old when I joined up. I, like everyone else, spent six weeks learning how to be a soldier. During this time it was discovered that I was a square peg and the army only seemed to have round holes!

It took four months to find a suitable square hole in the shape of the Army School of Hygiene. Since I was already a Sanitary Engineer/Inspector and a part-time teacher it seemed strange that it took so long to arrive at such an obvious solution.

One tends to think of war in terms of guns, bombs and torpedoes - killing and being killed - but there are many essential services that support the soldier at the front, the pilot in the air and the sailor at sea. Every fighting man must not only be fit when enters the service but he must be kept fit. Hygienic practices were all important in this area and I became a lecturer (with extra 4/9 per day).

At this time, 1943, the 6th Airborne Division was formed from volunteers. I volunteered and had to decide whether to be a glider or parachutist. The former would receive one shilling per day extra and the latter two shillings. I went for the Paras! After basic training we watched the men, one course ahead of us make their first jump - I joined the Gliders!

We were by now preparing for the second front and to look after 6,500 airborne troops, a unit of health experts was formed. It consisted of six Corporals, one Sergeant, one Staff Sergeant, one Lieutenant, one Major and in overall charge, was Colonel MacEwen, Director of Medical Services. The Colonel was a man who won instant respect - and that before we knew that he was a member of the brewing family!

On June 6th, 1944 I crossed the Channel on a naval barge, not by glider as I expected to do. I was Staff Sergeant with one Lance Corporal and a Private, one motorbike and a 15 cwt truck to make up our small unit. Half-way over one motor broke down and the sailors manning the barge struggled hard to keep on course. We landed, but several hours late, which was fortunate for us as the Commandos had cleared the landing zone.

The sight that lay before us was one that has been described many times by many people in books and on film but no-one who was not there can know the impact it made - the smell - the noise and the fear bred a determination to fight the influences of evil that lay behind it all.

We went to work immediately to find water supplies - ponds and streams to purify them as, in retreat, the Germans had, whenever possible, poisoned them. At times we got too close to the retreating Germans for comfort so we became very efficient at digging slit trenches. Training troops to be self-sufficient and teaching them that hygienic habits are all important even under fire and should be observed whenever possible is not always easy. But we had no outbreaks of dysentry or malaria so we only had to fight the enemy.

Normandy is a farming area and many of the ponds were used by cattle to drink from so we soon had complaints from farmers. To change the habits of a herd of cows is not easy so they had reactions to our anti-malarial sprays. We were soon forgiven, however, and local people welcomed us and helped wherever possible. It was rewarding for us to be made so welcome.

For three months I was only fractionally behind the front line doing what I had been trained to do - often frightened beyond belief, and sometimes almost enjoying the contacts with the local people, but always encouraged by the comradeship that can only be appreciated by men with a common cause.

Of our entire unit we only lost three men - the Staff Sergeant damaged his back and returned to England, the Lieutenant was killed almost immediately on landing and the Major was shot after about a week trying to rescue a wounded man. He had been with us long enough for us to learn to respect him. We dug his grave in Ronville Churchyard and I made a cross out of the lead that had been blasted off the church roof. Years later I returned but found he had been re-buried in a war cemetery near by. It was the right thing to do but somehow I feel that his second funeral could not have generated the emotion of the first.

After three months I returned to England and was later sent out to the Far East - but that's another story.

Wilfred Twells

I was born in Shardlow and, apart from the war years, have lived there all my life.

I was called up, in the army, in July 1940, and after four months training in Scotland, was on active duty in various places around Britain, including defensive operations along the Thames estuary during the Battle of Britain. After about fourteen months in Britain, the next four years of my life was spent in the Far East.

The British 18th Division, of which my battalion of Sherwood Foresters was part, sailed from Liverpool in October 1941, originally bound for the Middle East. We sailed across the Atlantic Ocean, through enormous seas, arriving at Halifax harbour, Nova Scotia, where we transferred from the British troopships to American converted liner troopships, and sailed south to Trinidad, then eastwards to South Africa where, because Japan had entered the war by bombing the American naval base at Pearl Harbour, Hawaii, and invaded southern Thailand and northern Malaya, the division was diverted from the Middle East to Singapore.

One of the division's three brigades was sent directly across the Indian Ocean to Singapore and into almost immediate action in Malaya, while the remaining two brigades, which included my battalion, went first to India, where we trained and became partly acclimatised to the heat until, within three weeks, we too were sent to Singapore where, after only two weeks, during which the division took part in the battle of Singapore, the whole division, together with about eighty thousand other British, Australian, Indian and Malay troops, became prisoners of war, when the British Command, led by Lieutenant-General Arthur E Percival, surrendered Singapore Island to the Japanese.

Then followed three and a half years of what is described by Lord Russell of Liverpool, in his history of Japanese war crimes, The Knights of Bushido, as "the mass destruction, by starvation and forced labour, which turned tens of thousands of healthy men into diseased skeletons. POWs were driven like slaves, beaten, tortured and murdered by the Japanese and Korean guards and died in thousands from disease and malnutrition.".

Lord Russell's grim description of the ordeals suffered by Allied POWs, in particular of the building of the Burma/Siam railway by POWs and native workers, is taken from statements given by witnesses during the International War Crimes Trials, when many leading Japanese military and government officials, together with members of the Japanese armed forces, were sentenced to death or long prison sentences for atrocities committed against POWs.

Many, if not most, of those atrocities were committed during the fifteen months it took to build the railway, when sixteen thousand POWs died or were murdered, almost half of whom were British, mostly of the 18th Division.

Even after fifty years, I still feel the effects from my experiences and ordeals, of the abuse to my body caused by the harsh slavery, starvation and serious tropical ailments I suffered from. The memories are engraved on my mind.

Memories of helping to bury so many of my fellow POWs, reduced to emaciated, diseased men, yet still so young. And of the beatings, the degradations, the slavery of being made to work for twelve hours and more, in tropical heat, with little to drink, on starvation diets of rice and little else. Racked by malaria, beri-beri, dysentery, skin diseases of all kinds, including tropical ulcers which rotted the flesh down to the bone; and with no medication other than natural aids such as using shredded tobacco as poultices for minor ulcers and skin sores, with major ulcers treated by having the pus scraped out, after which boiling hot compresses were applied; a treatment which, while doing some good, caused the diseased and weakened man to scream with pain.

Memories of the cholera epidemic which I miraculously survived but during which my POW pal died an agonising and distressing death, together with two thirds of all the men in the camp, leaving those of us who survived just existing, mere skin and bone, yet still forced to work on, in nightmare conditions. Throughout much of South East Asia and Japan, British and Allied POWs suffered appalling atrocities, and the cruellest of treatment from Japan's military factions. Today, no doubt wanting to forget their countrymen's actions during the war, Japanese industries are flourishing in many of the nations of the world.

While such world-wide wars as the First and Second World Wars must never be allowed to destroy mankind ever again, atrocities such as the Japanese committed, and the Nazi's destruction of six million Jews during the Holocaust, must never be forgotten, but remain for ever a constant reminder of man's inhumanity to his fellow man.

Heather Chandler

Dedicated to R., one of many British Prisoners of War forced by the Japanese to work on building the infamous railway from Burma to India which crosses the bridge on the River Kwai. During this time R. fell sick with malaria and had a vision of Christ standing beside his bed. I felt very privileged to hear his story nearly fifty years ago.

River Crossing
Cradled in aching limbs he lay
shivering in a furnace of despair.
Thunder and heartbeat mingled
pumped sweat with drenching rain
leaving him parched and hopeless
beached at the edge of consciousness.

This was the price they had to pay
for the railway on the River Kwai.
Charon asked no less
for ferrying the Styx.

Raindrops skittered
on the palm-thatched roof
a rustling reminder
of childhood woods near home.

Memory must be held close
for little else is left ...
            ...Spring meadows
            Summer buzzed gardens
            Autumn's ripe orchards
            and Winter Christmasses
            - sweet voices carolling
            to the Child in the manger
            and a stained glass figure
            offering benediction.
            Images streaming in sunlight
            flit like mosquitoes in the mind....
                    CHRIST IN GLORY comes
                    to stand beside his prison bed.
As the fever breaks he has no doubt
that Faith one day will take him home.

Joyce Woodhouse

I like many others recall VE Day with joy. It was special, as it was my sixteenth birthday. I remember quite clearly Frank Smith leading a torch-light procession from Coalville with youngsters and other age groups eight abreast, linking arms and singing all the way through Whitwick. More joined in up Leicester Road to a field facing the Forest Rock public house. We gathered round a massive bonfire, singing and dancing. It certainly was A Day to Remember.

The Billet

In February 1940 the first edition of The Billet was produced. In an introductory article its purpose was described thus:

WHAT THE BILLET STANDS FOR

A message to the Services

If you look in your dictionary you will find the word `billet' means amongst other things, a small paper, a short note. This will explain the first purpose of this little production. It will be a link from home with those who are away, giving items of news, gossip and humour from Coalville and district. The second aim is just as important. It is to tell the people at home how you are progressing. With your help The Billet may weld us into one big family. In brief, we want to exchange news and views with you'

The Billet was produced by Jack Hussey (late Leicestershire Regiment) and The Leicester Mercury. It cost two pence at home and was free to the Forces. Goodwill messages were received from many celebrities of the time, including Gracie Fields, Richard Dimbleby, Jack Warner and Betty Driver of Coronation Street fame. Apart from members of the Forces and those at home, The Billet included contributions form Wombo who penned many verses, Nobby who seemed to have an inexhaustible supply of jokes and Thomas Woolman whose cartoons were featured in many editions. The massive task of distribution to the Forces was in the hands of the `Unknown Lady' whose identity was only revealed, in September 1945, to be Mrs Dorothy Harris of Bakewell Street, Coalville. Mrs Harris also turned out to be Nobby. Wombo was the pen name of Mr G N Burrows of Ashby Road, Coalville.

In January 1946, The Billet prepared to say good-bye:

It is with a great deal of regret that we announce that The Billet must soon end its successful run. The final issue will be published in March next, with the 75th number.

We are sorry that is it impossible to accede to the request of hundreds in the Services to continue publication until they are demobilised in months and years to come.

The Billet was essentially a war effort, and we feel pride in the fact that it has gone from success to success. This is due in no small measure to the whole-hearted support we have received from all quarters.

Now that the war is ended the need for The Billet is not so acute, although we do appreciate the requests from Servicemen and women to continue production, even when they return to civilian life.

The theme of many letters is: "The Billet must never be allowed to cease publication; we must make it a magazine for Coalville Servicemen and women in peace time."

It was never our intention to nurse The Billet to become a Coalville newspaper. It is much too precious. We have tried to make The Billet a link between those in the Services and the folk at home and we believe we have been successful.

In the short time remaining, we shall be happy to hear from friends in the Forces and at home.

The last edition in March 1946 contained an appreciation from the printers, A.T. Shelley & Co., Albion Hill, Leicester, which contained a threatening P.S. - If this contribution is blue-pencilled we will not print the final Number (75).

THE BILLET.

COALVILLE'S NEWS MAGAZINE FOR THE FORCES AND HOME FRONT.

Another entry for the "NOBBY" Competition sent by R. L. Laywood, formerly of Bridge Road, Coalville.

THE V SIGN.

THE topic of Coalville is, of course, the V sign. Some regard it as merely a stunt, others as the hall-mark of genius in publicity.

We leave it to all of you to argue as to its merits, merely mentioning it to record that Coalville took part in a campaign regarded as one of our major propaganda successes abroad.

The V sign has been plastered all over the town and underground, too, as tubs of coal coming up from the mines bore the ensign of victory.

People out shopping gave the familiar · · · — in making purchases, and a dog was seen in the street with a V on its back !!

The "V" Puppy.—A month-old shepherd dog puppy, with a perfectly-shaped "V" in white on a jet black forehead, has been born at the farm of Mr. J. Chadwick, Donington-le-Heath.

Americans at Monastery. — A party of convalescent American soldiers and airmen recently visited Mount St. Bernard Trappist Monastery.

Boxer's Death.—Ben Foord, the former British and Empire heavy-weight boxing champion, was found shot dead at his home in South Africa. Foord was well-known in the Coalville district. He married Miss Phyllis Sowter, of Ashby-de-la-Zouch, who was a teacher at Ellistown School. He defeated Jack Petersen at Leicester for the British and Empire titles on August 17th, 1936, Petersen being beaten by a technical knock-out in the third round. Foord, in obtaining the victory, badly injured his right hand, and lost his titles to Tommy Farr in London soon after.

British Restaurant. — The British Restaurant at Coalville, which has a capacity of 300 meals a day, supplied 862 meals during the first week. The number attending on the first day was 85, and this increased to 174 on Wednesday.

Miners Top Again.—Leicestershire is the only coalfield to obtain an output bonus for March. Since the bonus scheme started Leicestershire has never failed to earn a bonus, and the local miners are the only ones with such a grand record.

Miners' Holiday.—For the first time in history Leicestershire miners had a week's holiday with pay, and it was well-deserved. Unfortunately for many of the miners there was a shortage of beer.

B.B.C. AND "THE BILLET."

The B.B.C. gave "The Billet" a pat on the back after the nine o'clock news on the General Forces programme on Friday, July 14th.

A commentator said, "I expect many of you have heard of 'The Billet,' the Coalville magazine which has been sent out free to local men and women in the Forces every month since February, 1940, and which follows them all over the world."

"The current issue tells how a copy was dropped by plane behind the Jap lines in Burma for a Coalville boy serving with the Chindits."

"I met Jack Hussey, the editor, the other day, and he told me that the magazine has contributed over £200 to the Coalville Troops Comforts Fund."

"NOBBY" AND ME
POOR MAJOR

Sentry: "Afraid I can't let you go by without the password, sir."

Major: "But confound you I tell you I've forgotten it. You know me well enough. I'm Major Jones."

Sentry: "Can't help it, sir. Must have password."

Voice from tent: "Oh, don't stand there arguing all night, Bill. Shoot 'im.'

A BITTER PILL FOR HITLER.

Coalville & District War Weapons Week realised £237,129. (See page 2)
[*Drawn by Mr. Thos. Woolman, Belvoir rd., Coalville*

It was his first attempt at rifle practice, and with his opening shot he scored a bull. But the other nine shots did not even leave a mark on the target.

"How do you account for these misses?" snapped the sergeant. "That first one must have been beginner's luck!"

"Sorry, sergeant," apologised the recruit. "I thought I had to get all the bullets through the same hole."

ONE GUESS

"Heard from your Tom lately, Mrs. Smith?"

"Yes, I'd a letter the other day. I don't know whether he's in Iceland or in Libya, but he says he's been bitten by a camel."

The new recruit was a simple-looking lad from the country, so the sergeant thought he would pull his leg a bit. "Here, my lad," he said, "let's see how far you can climb up that searchlight beam."

"Ah, you can't catch me," said the recruit. "I know that trick. As soon as I get half-way up you'll turn out the light."

IT DOESN'T PAY

Worker in a war factory took several days off and at the end of the week was surprised to find a handful of German marks in his pay-envelope.

With the marks was a note: "This is your reward for not working When you don't work, you work for the enemy!"

ENGLISH—AS SPOKEN BY SOME AT COALVILLE.

There have been stories of Coalville boys meeting overseas, often in the dark, through one hearing the other talk in a way peculiar to Coalville. Some people say Coalville has no dialect, compared with London, Tyneside or Lancashire, but the following expressions, often heard in Coalville, are of interest and we hope they will raise a smile.

ENYEERDOTE—Have you heard anything?
FETCHUNOMMER—Fetch a hammer.
OWYERMEMON—How are you, my man?
STREETDOWN STRAIGHT—Straight down the street.
ENYERGOINWHOM—Are you going home?
ERZABADUN—She is a bad one.
AYSCORTAROT—He has caught a rat.
PITS PLEEING THRAY DEES—Pit is playing three days,
    i.e., the pit is closed down for three days.
SHAYWUNNER—She won't.
AYDUNNER—He doesn't.
ENYER SANE MA, DUG, AYZA BLACK UN WEE A LUNG
    TEEL.—Have you seen my dog. He is a black one
    with a long tail.

THEY SOLD THEIR SHIRTS

At a vegetable auction sale at Ellistown, for the Hotel Comforts for the Forces Fund, miners and others, towards the end of the sale, pulled off their ties, shirts and vests, which were sold by the auctioneer. Fortunately, the purchasers returned shirts to the men after the sale, which realised £36 15s.

100 Mile Hitch-hike.—A 15-year-old London girl, with another girl of the same age, previously billeted in Coalville as an evacuee, ran away from their London homes and hitch-hiked to Coalville. They were taken back by their parents.

Boxing.—A good crowd enjoyed a boxing tournament between Ashby and Hinckley Amateur Boxing Clubs at the Baths Hall, in aid of the Red Cross. Supt. R. Bullimore said boxing was part of the training of the Ashby A.T.C., but after a successful tournament with Coalville A.T.C., the Ashby officers refused to allow their boys to box in public. Following this the Ashby club was formed and had raised over £300 for charity.

British Restaurant. — The British Restaurant at Coalville, which has a capacity of 300 meals a day, supplied 862 meals during the first week. The number attending on the first day was 85, and this increased to 174 on Wednesday.

Hermit.—A remarkable character, George Eadon, has died in a hovel near Ibstock. Known as "Soldier George" he lived for the last 20 of his 66 years as a hermit.

Firemens' Lament

Fire watchers, fire parties, A.F.S.,
  WHO'S joining next, you'll never guess,
The time is coming I'll be bound,
  When there won't be nearly enough
                fires to go round.

Patiently Goering, his corpulent nibs,
  Loads up his Dorniers with magnesium
                squibs,
But our amateurs here, all ready to pounce,
  Don't give the fizzlers time to bounce.

We regular firemen, standing by,
  See the flares light up the sky.
Get prepared, and then we're told,
  All the fires have been controlled.

Fire engines shining, ready to go,
  Hoping to be in on a really big show,
Phone bells ring, gum boots clump,
  Auxiliaries gone, with their trailer pump.

Incendiaries tackled by women and kids,
  With bags of sand and dustbin lids,
Wardens, firemen, spotters and so on,
  Don't leave a fireman much to go on.

Once we could call one fire our own,
  They kept it burning for us alone,
Someone should tell them, they ought to
                know,
  We're all dressed up and nowhere to go.
                WOMBO, A.F.S.

CAUGHT NAPPING.

During a dance at Thringstone House Club the music stopped suddenly and the 200 dancers were told that prizes would be given to all who could produce their gas masks within a minute. Only one of the company, Audrey Smith, of Osgathorpe, had brought a gas mask, and she won the prize.

Home Guard "Stands Down." —Coalville Home Guard, with a record second to none in the area, presented a smart appearance on the "stand down" parade. These men, who rallied to the country's call, can now relax, knowing that they did a good job well.

COALVILLE NOW LIT UP.
Members of Coalville Urban Council reversed their decision not to light the street lamps, which are now shining as far as the regulations permit. There were many protests against the Council's original decision, and the question was reconsidered at a special meeting.

PRISON CAMP PLAY.—Sergt.-Major J. Hannigan, of Coalville, sent this picture of British prisoners of war in a play at their prison camp in Germany. They made the scenery and costumes mainly of paper.

L/Bdr. L. F. Taylor writes from the Western Front: For the past 4½ years I have received " The Billet " regularly every month, and, like all the local boys, simply devour its contents, but to-day I had the biggest thrill of all, as I got my first issue of " The Billet " since coming overseas. I cannot possibly express all my feelings of thanks to you and the " Unknown Lady " in getting this grand paper out to all our local boys and girls all over the world. I'm proud to say we played our part in the Battle of Britain, and in Jerry's latest nuisance, the flying bomb, and now I think we have come to the last job of quietening the Germans for good. Please give my best wishes to all my friends, and again thanks for " The Billet." May the Victory Number come soon.

Escaped From Japs

A Coalville soldier, Fusilier George Ballard, of Charles-street, who, three years ago, was a prisoner in the hands of the Japanese, and after being bound with rope, was flung into a bungalow and left to perish in a blazing village, has returned home on leave.

With 25 members of his regiment taken prisoner, Fusilier Ballard lay helpless in the bungalow in the midst of battle. They were bound together in a human chain, and then, to their horror, they found the village was on fire. Their Japanese guards ran away and left the prisoners to their fate, but after desperate struggles they managed to loosen their bonds and make a dash for liberty.

" THE BILLET " RE-UNITES SCHOOL FRIENDS AFTER 23 YEARS.

May we remind local boys who may get to New Zealand that a welcome awaits them at the home of Mr. and Mrs. Will Maunders, 176, High-stret, Rangiora, Canterbury, New Zealand, who will be happy to entertain them. Mr. and Mrs. Maunders, who receive " The Billet," formerly lived at Hugglescote. If you get to Port Littleton, just ask for " Bill " Maunders.

By the way, when we first published this address in May, 1944, Sergt. Frank Birt, of Hugglescote, who is serving overseas, recognised that he knew Mr. and Mrs. Maunders, and wrote to them. Not only did they send him a grand parcel, but they also gave him their son's address, with the result that Sergt. Birt and " Bill " Maunders, jun., school pals at Hugglescote, got into touch with each other for the first time for 22 years.

"THE BILLET" GETS TO TOBRUK

ELLISTOWN BOY'S GRATITUDE

The gallant boys at Tobruk, whose courage and endurance stirred all our hearts, were able to read "The Billet" in their grim struggle.

This is revealed to us in a letter from Mrs. M. Woolerton, of Midland-road, Ellistown, who says: In your November issue there was a letter from my husband, L/Cpl. C. Woolerton. At the time he wrote the letter to you he was unable to disclose where he was stationed. I thought that readers of your grand little paper would like to know that for $4\frac{1}{2}$ months he was in Tobruk. I wonder if any other local lads were there. My husband did not meet any boys from this district until July, when, in Egypt, he met an old friend, Marine D. Billings, of Whitwick. They were able to spend four days together before Marine Billings moved on. Marine Billings wrote to tell me that he and my husband had a lot to talk about and that my husband was actually in Tobruk last January.

MET IN PALESTINE

Sergt. Leslie Eoot, of Park-road, has met Albert Beasley, of Albert-road, in Palestine. He also came across another Coalville man named Richards, whose parents live in London-road, Coalville.

"THE BILLET" by Dispatch Rider

One of our boys tells us that recently when on duty the Sergt. Major told him there was a letter for him at the Company Office and that it had been brought by a dispatch rider from headquarters. Told by the Sgt. Major to fetch it he found on arrival at the office that it was 'The Billet.'

FROM A NAZI CAMP.

A Coalville Broom Leys school teacher. Miss Monica Weston, who recently returned from the German frontier. where she had been interned in a Nazi camp since December. 1940, in an interview told of the appalling conditions under which the internees live.

She said there were over 1,000 women in the camp and nearly 300 children. They could not live on the scanty rations supplied by the Nazis. and it was only the food parcels supplied by the British Red Cross which kept them alive.

There were no sanitary conditions in the camp. the food was wretched. and the beds of double-decker type. with straw mattresses. Vermin crawled all over the rooms. The internees did all their own work in the camp. which was surrounded by barbed wire and guarded by German soldiers.

"The Billet" Enquiry Bureau

Relations and friends of members of the Forces who require information are invited to use 'The Billet' Enquiry Bureau. Hundreds of people have been helped by this free service. If you require advice, write or call at 53, Belvoir Road, Coalville.

Cousins Meet.—L.A.C. Raymond Springthorpe, of 44, Silver-street, Whitwick, was sitting in a cinema in Iraq, and at the end of a picture, turned round to see his cousin, Aircraftman Leonard Springthorpe, of 60, Kingsmead-road, Knighton, sitting just behind him. They had last met in England, two years ago, and had no idea they were serving near each other.

Heard Husband's Voice From Cairo.—In the greetings recently broadcast from Cairo, Mrs. Storer, of Stapleton, heard the voice of her husband, Mr. S. Storer, who is in the Tanks Corps. He was also heard by his parents at Heather.

SHORT STORIES
OF COALVILLE'S PART IN THE WAR

B.E.F. Memories. — In 1939, a Coalville boy, with the B.E.F. in France, entered a cafe, and in his best French, ordered three brandies. He received three plates of fried eggs! Another Coalville boy smartly saluted a man in French uniform, to receive the reply, in good English, "Thank you, sir, but I'm only the postman."

Norway. — Coalville and district boys, mainly Territorials, were in the fighting in Norway. Their stories are epics of courage and endurance, under terrble conditions, in the absence of supporting aircraft.

Dunkirk.—Coalville boys were amongst the 350,000 men brought safely back from France. They lost equipment, and arrived with their battle-dress almost in rags.

Blood-Stained "Billet." — In the hell of Dunkirk, a local soldier picked up a copy of "The Billet" on the battlefield. It was stained with blood, and although the soldier lost two fingers, he managed to bring home this copy of "The Billet" and his pay book.

The Relatives.—"The Billet" pays tribute to Coalville's brave parents who have been through so many anxious periods, waiting for news of their loved ones, and offers sympathy to those who are bereaved.

Gallant Act. — Sergt. Harry Wileman, of Coalville, although surrounded by Japanese, stayed for twenty-seven hours in the Burma rade who was eventually taken to safety. To relieve their parched throats they sucked bamboo leaves.

With the Desert Tanks. —We had first-hand information in 1941 of life in the desert. Local boys told us how they tossed coins for the privilege of having a bath, and how officers and men took the same chance.

In Tobruk. — The gallant boys of Tobruk, whose courage and endurance stirred all hearts, were able to read 'The Billet" during their grim struggle. This was told to us by Cpl. C. Woolerton.

In Malaya. — Pte. T. Wells wrote to us in 1941 saying how much the local boys in Malaya enjoyed reading "The Billet."

In Malta.—Coalville boys took their part in manning the guns at Malta, which had over 1,000 raids, including 250 in six weeks, and L/Bdr. A. Storer wrote to say how "The Billet" always got through, and how he and Gnr. J. R. Greasley enjoyed reading it between the raids.

News of Prisoners. — In July, 1941, we received news from Bdr. Ernest Mountain, a prisoner of war in Germany. He told us how he was using a large room as a barber's shop, and how they had formed a dance orchestra. Later other prisoners told us of other camp activities, including stage shows.

Marooned on Desert Island.— After being marooned on an uninhabited island, following ten days adrift in an open boat, with only rice and cocoanuts to eat, after a long period of day and night fighting in jungle swamps, infested with snakes and crocodiles, L.-Cpl. Fred Grice returned home to tell us how he escaped from Singapore. L/Cpl. Grice has since been killed in action.

Under Jerry's Nose.—Pte. E. Hammonds wrote from C.M.F.: "I am writing this in a house right under Jerry's nose. We dare not leave in the daytime. In spite of all this, I receive 'The Billet.'"

Greetings from Prison Camps. —In 1941 we received a number of Christmas cards from local men in Nazi prison camps, as well as from boys and girls in the Services stationed in various parts of the world.

Axis Cracked in North Africa. —Tpr. F. Barkby told us in 1943 how the Axis cracked in North Africa, and of the great welcome the Allies had in Tunis. He said the mopping-up was a sight for sore eyes. Thousands of Germans and Italians gave themselves up without any trouble, driving their own vehicles, which were packed.

Iceland. — In 1940, Coalville boys serving in Iceland, over 1,000 miles from home, received their copies of "The Billet," which re-united two Coalville friends, who were serving there, unknown to each other.

In the Holy Land.—The Rev. L. A. Fereday, a former Coalville minister, wrote us in 1940 from the Holy Land, where he was a chaplain. He sent greetings, and said Coalville boys there prayed regularly for the people of Coalville.

Brought Down Raider.—Sergt. Eric Neal, when only 20 years of age, brought down an enemy raider over the Channel, although he was wounded, his turret jammed and his radio out of action. Later Sergt. Neal was reported missing, after receiving the D.F.M.

In Action in Greece. — A.C. George Massey took part in the fighting in Greece in 1941, and before his 21st birthday had probably seen as much of battle as some of the old soldiers of the last war.

With Free French.—In 1942, L.A.C. P. Finney, of Coalville, was serving with the Free French, and in a letter described some thrilling experiences, and said he got on very well with the French airmen.

"Billet" By Plane.—Cliff Higham, when in the Middle East, told us how "The Billet" was dropped to him by plane whilst he was serving in the sandy wastes.

Girls Fly With the R.A.F.— In 1942 we heard from three local girls, Kath Biddle, Sarah Hanningan and A.C.W.1 Payne, all flight mechanics in the W.A.A.F., stating how they serviced planes and accompanied pilots on flights to test the repairs.

Libya Battle.—Cpl. E. Woolerton wrote in 1942 giving some idea of the fighting and conditions in the desert battles, and told a graphic story of a tank battle.

Money to Burn in Desert.—In the desert in 1942, Coalville boys captured a huge quantity of notes from the Italians. They thought the notes were of no value, and used them to light their cigarettes and the camp fires. Then, a few days later, they reached a town to discover the notes they had burnt were genuine. Bdr. Billy Lowe, the Coalville boxer, told us the story.

In the Desert. — Coalville boys taking part in General Wavell's great advance in 1940, praised the British people at home for their calmness and courage during the Battle of Britain.

Desert Beetle Racing. — In July, 1942, Trumpeter Reg. Carter sent us an interesting letter describing beetle racing in the desert, and stating how, in the sandy wastes, boys backed the favourite with fag ends.

Girl Bombed at Sea.—Pte. Dorothy B. Bowler, serving in Nairobi, was twice bombed on her way out.

How "Jerry" Ran. — How German troops near the Siene ran so fast that our troops could not catch them, was described by Lieut. S. Hammond, who was the first Leicestershire man to cross the Siene.

In Abyssinia.—Tom Findley and E. Smith wrote to say how much "The Billet" meant to them in the wilds of Eritrea.

Prisoners Return.—Many local men came home from Nazi prison camps in time to hear the news of the end of the European War.

'BLOOD, SWEAT AND TEARS'

With the Gurkhas. — Having been thrilled by stories of the famous Indian Regiment, the Gurkhas, we were pleased to hear from Lieutenant Hall, of Ellistown, that he had been posted to this splendid native regiment. Lieutenant Hall had previously served in India.

Battle of Britain.—Coalville pilots, crews and ground staffs helped in smashing Nazi attacks in the Battle of Britain, when in six days 500 Nazi bombers were sent crashing to destruction.

Home From Malta. — Cpl. Cyril Allen, who was in Malta during the great siege, told us, when on leave, of some of the terrific air raids and of life on the island.

Tobruk Battle.—Coalville boys were in the battle for Tobruk, and in March, 1942, Pte. R. Staley, of Hugglescote, in a description of the battle, with shells falling day and night, said the British boys attacked till all they had, and never did one draw back.

Crossing the Line.—Many of Coalville's sons serving in the Royal Navy, took part in the famous crossing the line ceremony, when those who had not previously been over the Equator were the unfortunate victims of the ducking ceremony. C.P.O. O. A. Chambers gave us an interesting description, and A.B. Jack Starkey sent us photographs.

With Natives in Jungle. — Life amongst the natives of West Africa, who still use poisoned arrows and spears when hunting, and hold dances to the beat on tom-toms every evening, was described by L.A.C. Roy Humphries.

Visit to Gold Mine.—L.A.C. Andrew Wilkins visited a gold mine in India, where he was allowed to hold a brick worth £12,000.

In Whale Hunt.—L/Bdr. Tom Kelham told of taking part in a whale hunt on a lonely North Atlantic island, when a cry of "Grinda" brought all the islanders to the sea front for the "kill."

A Ghost Town.—"It was like walking into a ghost town. There was no one about, and the town was flattened." This description of a landing in Burma was given by Gnr. H. L. Greasley.

Saw Duisburg Die.—F/Sergt. Smallwood, describing the great attack on Duisburg, said: "The sky was littered with planes crawling like wasps, and below there were various types of ack-ack fire from this most heavily defended city. I looked over Duisburg as the first bomb fell, and later saw it vanish like a ghost under the heaviest bombardment I had ever been on."

The Frozen Orange.—Sergt. Smallwood, who in 1945 shot down a jet propelled fighter, took an orange on one of his bombing trips in 1944, and when he got back from over enemy country, the orange was covered with a quarter of an inch of ice.

Children Rescued From Raft. —A.B. Jack Starkey told us in in 1945 how he assisted in the rescue of 17 people, including four young children, who had been adrift on a raft in mid-ocean for three weeks, with huge man-eater sharks following them day and night.

The BILLET

World Peace Number

No. 69   SEPTEMBER, 1945   Price 2d.

THIS COPY OF **World Peace Number of "The BILLET"**
WAS ISSUED TO COMMEMORATE
THE FINAL VICTORY of the UNITED NATIONS
AUGUST, 1945.

And was purchased by ....

Community Leisure Services presents

EVENTS TO COMMEMORATE THE 350TH ANNIVERSARY OF THE ENGLISH CIVIL WAR IN ASHBY DE LA ZOUCH 17 - 25 JUNE 1995

Date	Time	Event	Venue
17 June	7.30 pm	Make Haste Home A Civil War Play with humour	Venture Theatre
19-25 June	Various	Big Top Tour '95 Travelling Theatre Events	Bath Grounds
20-25 June	Various	Living History Encampment	Ashby Castle
24 June	12 Noon	Uneasy Lies the Crown - A Play	Ashby Castle
	3.00-4.30 pm	The Siege of Ashby Castle (1643)	Castle & Memorial Grounds
	6.30 pm	The Arrival of King Charles I from Naseby	Market Street
	7.30 pm	17th Century Entertainment Music from Strawhead Folk Band	Hood Park Leisure Centre
	7.30 pm	Officers Banquet	Lyric Rooms
25 June	11.00 am	Uneasy Lies the Crown - A Play	Ashby Castle
	1.15 pm	Street Battle	Market Street
	3.00-4.30 pm	The Seige of Ashby Castle (1646) including Battle and Surrender	Ashby Castle & Memorial Grounds

Ashby Museum Exhibition of Civil War artifacts, costumes and model of Ashby Castle open Easter to September.

For further information on the above events, please contact Mr Goff Lewis on 01530 833333 Ext. 382

NORTH WEST LEICESTERSHIRE DISTRICT COUNCIL

DIRECT LEISURE SERVICES

 Direct Leisure Services manage the Hermitage and Hood Park Leisure Centres on behalf of North West Leicestershire District Council.

Swimming, Children's Soft Play, After School Coaching, Fitness classes including Aerobics, Step, Slide and Box-a-Cise are part of the programme as well as Tea Dances, Sequence Dances, 50+ Sessions, Special Needs and Ladies Leisure.

A wide and varied range of activities are on offer at both facilities covering the needs of all ages within the community.

■■■■■■■■■■ HOOD PARK LEISURE CENTRE ■■■■■■

North Street
Ashby de la Zouch
Leicestershire LE65 1HU
Tel. 01530 412181

Hood Park Leisure Centre in Ashby de la Zouch is the focal point for sport in Ashby. Regular activities at the centre include the staging of Triathlons, Road Races, Dog Shows, Antique Fairs, Children's Parties and Musical Evenings.

A rare Outdoor Heated Swimming Pool is sited at Hood Park which is open from May to September attracting visitors from accross the Midlands.

Other facilities include a 4 Court Sports Hall, Fitness Suite, Sunbeds, Croquet Lawn and Floodlit All Weather Area. The Bar and Function Room is available for private parties.

■■■■■■■■■■HERMITAGE LEISURE CENTRE ■■■■■■

Silver Street
Whitwick
Leicestershire LE67 5EU
Telephone: 01530 811215

Hermitage Leisure Centre in Whitwick is one of the region's finest venues for top class events. International Table Tennis, World Class Snooker, National Orchestral Concerts, Trade Exhibitions, Dog Shows and Sporting Tournaments have all been successfuly staged at the centre.

A wide range of facilities are on offer inlcuding a 25m Swimming Pool, 6 Court Sports Hall, Fitness Suite, Health Suite with jacuzzi, sauna, steam room and sunbeds, Dance Studio and Floodlit Astroturf Courts.

NORTH WEST LEICESTERSHIRE
DISTRICT COUNCIL

Extensive facilities available at

CASTLE DONINGTON COMMUNITY COLLEGE

Use us for:

Parties	Licensed Bar	Village Arts
Seminars	Hall/Stage	Sports Field
Presentations	Gymnasium	Outdoor Pool
Fund Raising		
Meetings	Trim Trail	Training for Young People
Receptions	Bouncy Castle	
Interest Groups	Meeting/Seminar	Fitness Studio
Shows	Rooms	All Weather Pitches
Workshops		
Sports	Bowl's Mats	
Societies	Tennis Courts	Creche
Groups		

Resources include:- photocopier, computers, printing, audio/visual equipment, OHPs and a great deal more.

Think of Castle Donington Community Centre first. We're on your doorstep and we will do our best to be as helpful as possible. For further information call in at our reception or telephone 01332 810528. Details of the above facilities, Adult Classes, affiliated groups and societies can be obtained by asking for Peter Gerrard, Vice Principal.

Castle Donington Community College, Mount Pleasant, Castle Donington, Derby DE74 2LN.
Telephone: (01332) 810528
Leicestershire County Council - Education Department
North West Leicestershire District Council - First for Leisure Services.

Subscribers:

Ibstock Parish Council

Kenneth M. Butcher, accountant, Loughborough

Dave Collins, Education, Training & Careers Advisor, Coalville Technical College.